"This is a fabulous book! *Your Girl* is not only touching, it is teaching! Vicki's approach is biblical, straightforward, and relevant. A must read for every daughter's mother."
—Beth Moore, author, speaker, and founder of Living Proof Ministries

"Vicki's fingertips are on the pulse of every mother's heart across this nation as captured so effectively in the book *Your Girl*. Vicki has penned clear directions for anyone who wants to raise a daughter to make a difference in this world for Jesus. I am so thrilled to have this book as a resource to recommend to all the mothers I teach across this nation."
—Jackie Kendall, author of best-selling book *Lady in Waiting*

"Not only does Vicki Courtney tell it like it *should* be—she tells us how what *should* be, CAN be in practical, powerful ways. *Your Girl* is a must-read for every mother raising a daughter of any age."
—Nancy Rue, author of the Lily series for girls

"Vicki Courtney opens our eyes and empowers mothers by reminding us that we *do* still have tremendous influence in the lives of our daughters, that daughters are watching and listening for direction. *Your Girl* gives help and encouragement to equip mothers to navigate the culture and lead their daughters into maturity, rather than to allow the culture to take them by the hand and lead them through life."
—Nancy Stafford, co-star of "Matlock," speaker, and author of *Beauty by the Book: Seeing Yourself as God Sees You*

"Vicki's words will capture every mother's heart raising a daughter in today's world. *Your Girl* will encourage you to stand firm on God's promises and take back what we've allowed our society to creep into our homes."

—Terry Brown, creator of *TodaysGirls*

"I love this book. This is the book moms and mentors have been searching for. So timely, so right on, so real. Every woman with a heart to reach this generation of girls needs this book. It's one more powerful tool in the hands of God's girl movement. Vicki, we're singing the same song. Way to go girl."

—Lisa Ryan, co-host "700 Club," author, and speaker

Your Girl

Vicki Courtney

Your Girl

BROADMAN
& HOLMAN
PUBLISHERS

NASHVILLE, TENNESSEE

0-8054-3053-9

Published by Broadman & Holman Publishers
Nashville, Tennessee

Dewey Decimal: 248.843
Subject Heading: WOMEN \ MOTHERS \ VIRTUE

Unless otherwise stated, all Scripture quotations are
from NIV, the Holy Bible, New International Version, copyright © 1973, 1978, 1984 by International BIble Society.
Other versions include: NLT, Holy Bible, New Living
Translation, copyright © 1996. Used by permission of
Tyndale House Publishers, Inc., Wheaton, IL 60189 USA. All
rights reserved.; NKJV, New King James Version, copyright
© 1979, 1980, 1982, Thomas Nelson, Inc., Publishers; and
KJV, King James Version.

3 4 5 6 7 8 9 10 09 08 07 06 05 04

Contents

Dedication

Paige,

The first thing I said when you were born was, "I got my girl!" In that first year I treated you like a living doll, changing your clothes several times a day and making sure you never left the house without a hair bow, even if it meant sticking it on your pretty bald head with a dab of Karo syrup! I wanted everyone to know that you were my girl, not to mention *a girl!*

Today, thirteen years later, you are still a living doll, and you are still my girl. However, I would be remiss to claim you for my very own. As much as I cherish and love you, it could never match the love God has for you. May you continue to grow in the knowledge that you are, above all, His girl.

BFF,
Mom

Acknowledgments

Keith, I have said it before and I will say it over and over again: I could never have followed through with God's call on my life had you not viewed it as your calling as well. You are my husband, editor, advisor, and most of all, my best friend. I love you!

Ryan, Paige, and Hayden, thank you for loving me for who I am. Like Dad, you have viewed my calling as a calling on the entire family. You have graciously excused my domestic and culinary inadequacies in the name of manuscript deadlines. We may not be the Cleaver family, but praise God, we laugh. We have been so very blessed, and we must never forget it.

Mom, like many mothers and daughters, we had our share of rough years. I am so glad that God is restoring to us "the years the locusts have eaten" (Joel 2:25). Thank you for being an incredible mother, grandmother, and most of all, my friend.

To my mother-in-love, (aka Memaw), thank you for being a faithful prayer warrior—I have felt it. Thanks also for raising your son to be a godly husband and father.

Kristi, Michelle, Shelley, and Joy, you have kept things running smoothly at Virtuous Reality Ministries so I can stick to my gifts, which are clearly *not* the administrative details! Thank you for your devotion to God's call.

Carolyn, you were my friend before you were my pastor's wife. Thank you for cheering me on when I felt like giving up. God had a plan, and you were part of it.

I appreciate the sincere devotion of Broadman & Holman to this project. God had placed this vision on my heart to write this book, yet I lacked a publisher and the time to find one. I committed it to prayer, and God allowed our paths to cross (more than once) for such a time as this.

Thank you to all the moms (with daughters) who encouraged me over the last several years to write this book. I was appointed to write the book, but the cry to change the culture belongs to us all.

To my Lord and Savior, Jesus Christ: You lifted me out of the slimy pit, out of the mud and mire, and set my feet on a rock. You gave me a firm place to stand and put a new song in my mouth. Thank You for taking the "mud" in my life and using it for Your good and glory. I will never stop singing about Your grace and mercy—You are my *everything*.

Introduction

The drama surrounding the birth of my second child should have been my clue that life would never be the same. On a Saturday afternoon, several days before my due date, I mentioned to my husband, Keith, that I was experiencing scattered contractions. He dismissed it as false labor and discouraged me from calling my doctor. We had made several unnecessary trips to the hospital before. Keith, no doubt, was having flashbacks of our last hospital visit where he got to sleep upright in a metal chair while they monitored my false contractions throughout the night.

By Saturday evening my contractions were coming more regularly, at a safe six minutes apart. Once again, Keith discouraged me from calling my doctor. As the contractions continued to close in, I trusted my instincts and called my doctor. Keith, still doubting, begrudgingly got into the car. After dropping off our two-year-old son at a friend's house, we began the thirty-minute drive to the hospital. The contractions were coming at a regular three minutes apart and had taken on a level of pain that was somewhat reminiscent of the final stages of labor with my first child. I made a note to self: banish husband to couch for remainder of marriage. By the time we neared the hospital, Keith had turned on the hazard lights and was running every red light. I'm not sure if the petrified look on his face was due to fear of my coming wrath or fear of delivering our second child on the highway.

Finally, my husband squealed into the emergency entrance of the hospital, and I was immediately whisked away in a wheelchair. Keith raced to park the car. I knew it was serious when the nurse bypassed the station where I was to fill out the obligatory mounds of paperwork and screamed, "I need to get her into a room!" No sooner than the nurse had put me in a bed, my water broke and my contractions were coming one on top of another. At that point I was consumed with only one thought. I wish I could say it was a thought concerning the fact that my husband might miss the birth of our second child while parking the car, but instead it boiled down to this: *Epidural! I want my epidural!*

Normally, I am one tough woman, but when it comes to natural childbirth and being an "earth woman," forget it. The epidural I had received prior to the birth of my first child had left me extolling the virtues of modern medicine. Now, during my second delivery, Keith finally made it into the room as the nurse was calmly reassuring me that both my doctor and the anesthesiologist were just down the hall with another patient. "You are next on their list. Don't worry, there is plenty of time for an epidural." No sooner than she had finished her sentence, she glanced over to check my progress and screamed, "Oh no! The baby is crowning!" With that, she looked at my husband (who was wiping his brow, still shaken from the car ride) and screamed, "Quick! Go find me a doctor!" Now, I don't know about you, but a panicked nurse who is relying on a panicked father to find a doctor is *not* reassuring.

I could hear my husband in the hallway stammering, "Uh, we need a doctor . . . my wife . . ." Before he could finish his sentence, in rushed a man wearing blue jeans and a button-down shirt. *Great,* I thought. *He's recruited a father out of the waiting room to deliver our child. I sure hope he's seen enough episodes of ER to pull this off.* The stranger barely had time to put on the sterile gloves before I made the final push. With that, he held my baby up and I heard my husband say, "It's a girl! We have a daughter!" I could hardly contain my joy as a smile covered my face.

The stranger in street clothes asked Keith to cut the cord, and I vaguely remember thinking, *If these two amateurs leave my beautiful princess with a three-inch outie, I'll never forgive them.* Sensing my panic, the stranger informed me that he was an obstetrician and had stopped by the hospital to check on patients before going out to dinner. After cutting the cord (leaving a beautiful innie, by the way), he handed my daughter over to the nurse, who wrapped her tightly in a blanket and laid her on my chest. Of course, my first thought was that she was the most beautiful thing I had ever seen. In truth, she looked more like a little blue Smurf, due to her fast trip through the birth canal. All the same, I counted ten fingers and ten toes, and winced at the piercing set of lungs that left no doubt as to who was in charge. After inspecting my princess, I looked up at Keith and said, "We have a daughter. I got my girl."

Drama over, right? Wrong. It was only just beginning. In that first year I would often stand over her crib and watch her while she slept. I would talk to God and plead with Him to spare her from some of the painful mistakes I had made during my growing up years. Would she love me? Would she even like me? Would we become lifelong friends? Would she come to love the God I serve? Sure, I had many of the same questions with the birth of my son, Ryan, but somehow, this was different. It would be Keith's responsibility to model to Ryan, as well as to our third child, Hayden, what it means to be a godly man. It would be *my* responsibility to model to Paige what it means to be a godly woman. Could I do it? Was I up for the task?

On a recent evening I stood again over her bed and watched my now thirteen-year-old princess sleep. Her crib has long since been replaced with a contemporary cast-iron daybed. Gone was the little girl with the soft blond curls. Lying before me that evening was a teenager with a wispy blonde ponytail, painted fingernails, and her head resting on a pillowcase that had been autographed by her cabinmates at summer camp. Many of the questions I had petitioned to God while standing over her crib in earlier years had been answered. Yes, she loves me. She even *likes* me and had recently told me that next to Christ, I am her best friend. Yes, she loves Jesus . . . for now. But what about tomorrow? And the next day? And the days to come? That evening I had some new questions. Could she stand firm against the fast-approaching tidal wave of a culture absent of virtue? Was I equipped for the arduous task of counteracting the culture? In the end, would I succeed in my call to raise my daughter to be a godly woman?

As I glanced around her room, most everything was different, yet a few things remained the same. My eighth-grade princess still clutched "Nanny Beth," her stuffed bear from infancy, and her mother still prayed. That evening my prayers took on a more urgent tone as I realized that two-thirds of the time she was to spend in my nest had already expired. She was slowly getting her wings, and she would soon take flight. Once again I was overwhelmed with the magnitude of the responsibility I had been given. With that thought, I knelt beside her bed and prayed over my little girl, "Thank you, Lord, for trusting me with this priceless treasure. May I be a model of strength and godliness to her as she grows more and more in Your likeness. May she come to love You more than life itself." Quietly, I got up and kissed her softly on the cheek and whispered one final plea: "Father, help me raise my daughter to be *Your girl.*"

Part One

PREPARING
FOR BATTLE

CHAPTER ONE

I Am Mother; Hear Me Roar!

I can't take it any longer. If I continue to be subjected to the lewd subtitles on the covers of women's fashion magazines every time I stand in the grocery store checkout line, I just may give up eating. "Whispers, Oohs or Yahoos—Wouldn't You Like to Know What He Thinks about Your Lovemaking Noise Level?" How about, "Make Him Lust for You—the Most Erotic Way to Unhook Your Bra and More Tantalize-Him Tricks" or "Sex on the Brain—What the Guys in Your Office Are Really Thinking." "His 126 Secret Sex Thoughts—the Dastardly Details Racing through His Mind Right Now!" "G-Spots, C-Spots, and Now, V-Spots." What's left? Have we made it through the alphabet yet? Have women become nothing more than sex-starved junkies looking for a fix? The focus of these articles is always the same: use your "lust-abilities" to get your man. Don't expect him to look your way unless you can belly dance in the bedroom or tantalize him with the latest snag-a-man technique.

Unfortunately, teen fashion magazines, which are targeted to young impressionable thirteen- to seventeen-year-old girls, are not much better. Examples of subtitles are: "Be a Guy Magnet," "Make the First Move . . . P.S. He's Waiting," "Get

That Guy! How to Give the 'Look of Love' Plus Three Other Tricks That'll Have Him Dying to Get Close to You," "Twenty-two Jeans That Scream 'Nice Butt!'" Or how about these: "Swimsuits That'll Make Him Say, 'Hel-lo!'" or "Kiss Him! How to Make the First Move." Another one is, "Best Bottoms for Your Butt: Tops That Tease and Please." Tease and please whom? No doubt, the magazines are a dream come true for every teenage boy in America with raging hormones.

Suffice it to say, I'm fed up with the negative influences of our culture on women. The magazines, however, are only part of the problem. Add television, movies, and music, and our daughters are bombarded with smut from the moment they wake up to the moment they go to bed. As someone who is in the trenches of ministry to preteen and teen girls, not to mention their mothers, I am witnessing firsthand the devastating consequences our provocative culture is having on women, both young and old.

I recall one devastated mother at a conference at which I spoke. She sobbed on my shoulder as she shared about a sleepover her middle school daughter had attended. The popular group of boys had called the girls in the middle of the night. *Nothing different from the middle-school sleepovers of my day*, I initially thought. Unfortunately, these boys had been surfing porn sites prior to calling the girls, and they wanted to try out their new knowledge of "phone sex." Not your average sleepover from my day. One at a time, the boys described in graphic detail what they would do to each girl, if ever given the opportunity. Don't think something like this cannot happen to your daughter. These were "church kids."

If this wasn't the final straw that led me to write this book, it may have been when Abercrombie & Fitch released a new line of thong underwear targeted at young girls, ages seven to fourteen. Printed on the front were messages like "eye candy" and "wink wink." Or, the last straw may have been the tank top I spotted while out shopping for my daughter, bearing the logo, "Made to tease . . . A cheap thrill product." It was a tiny size 7. No doubt, every pedophile's dream come true. Regardless of what the last straw was, I've had enough, and I'm willing to bet you have too. Clearly, you are a concerned and caring mother, or you would not have picked up this book.

For those of us who are committed to raising our daughters to be godly, virtuous young women, we have a daunting task before us. My generation was subjected to its share of negative messages, but nothing that compares to the constant barrage of negative messages our daughters endure today at the hands of television, movies, music, magazines, and the Internet. The negative messages in my day tended to come at the hands of a few groups that constituted the minority voice. Unfortunately, many of the groups that once had a minority voice have now become the popular voice of the day.

The good news is that Christians are the majority in this country. The bad news is that we have apparently lost our voice because we have become the *silent* majority. If something is not done to counteract the negative influences in our culture, I fear we could lose an entire generation of young women to the ways of the world. Let's not fool ourselves into thinking the damage will only be short-term. If we don't find our voice and use it to speak out against the negative influences of our culture, our daughters will be molded by the voice of the day. The resulting damage will produce fallout that will carry over into our daughters' marriages and into their motherhood, thus impacting generations to come.

Many well-meaning mothers have been caught off guard by the gradual and progressive downturn of the culture. For those who have recently awakened to a battle raging out of control and have determined something must be done, what is the next step?

When the Israelites were heading into battle, King David summoned the men of Issachar, who "understood the times and knew what Israel should do" (1 Chron. 12:32). Likewise, before we enter into battle, we must first gain a better understanding of "the times."

What Are "the Times"?

(WARNING: Reading the following statistics may lead you to add rapture practice to your daily "to do" list.)

Issues Facing Today's Families

- Half of all first marriages will end in divorce.[1]
- Born-again Christians are just as likely to have been divorced as are non-born-again adults. More than 90 percent of such born-again Christians experienced their divorce after becoming born-again.[2]
- Forty percent of children in the U.S. go to bed each night without having a biological father living in their home to tuck them in.[3]
- Almost half of all children will spend part of their years living in a single-parent home.[4]
- In 2000, 33 percent of all babies were born to unmarried women, compared to 3.8 percent in 1940.[5]
- Houses headed by unmarried partners (single fathers, single mothers, and gay couples) increased significantly, while—for the first time ever—houses headed by a married couple fell to below 25 percent of all households.[6]
- Thirty percent of Americans say drinking is a problem in their home.[7]
- According to NetValue, children spent 64.9 percent more time on pornography sites than they did on game sites in September 2000. Over one quarter (27.5 percent) of children age seventeen and under visited an adult Web site, which represents three million unique underage visitors. Of these minors, 21.2 percent were fourteen or younger, and 40.2 percent were female.[8]

- Sex is the number one searched for term on the Internet today.[9]
- Adult bookstores now outnumber McDonald's restaurants in the U.S. by a ratio of 3:1.[10]
- Two out of every three shows on TV contain sexual content.[11]

Issues Directly Facing Our Daughters

- The number one wish for girls ages eleven to seventeen is to be thinner.[12]
- One study of Saturday morning toy commercials found that 50 percent of commercials aimed at girls spoke about physical attractiveness, while none of the commercials aimed at boys referred to appearance.[13]
- Thirty percent of high school seniors reported having at least five drinks in a row in the previous two weeks.[14]
- Twenty-five percent of high school seniors reported using illicit drugs in the past thirty days.[15]
- Nationwide, 46 percent of students in grades nine through twelve have had sex.[16]
- Fourteen percent of all thirteen-year-olds have had sex.[17]
- Nearly 35 percent of all young women in the U.S. become pregnant at least once before reaching the age of twenty—almost 850,000 each year.[18]
- Approximately 1.5 million U.S. women with unwanted pregnancies choose abortion each year.[19]
- Eighty-three percent of teens say that moral truth depends on the situation.[20]
- Dating on college campuses is all but obsolete, having been replaced by a "hookup" culture, where a guy and a girl get together for some form of physical encounter (ranging from kissing to having sex) with no expectation of anything further.[21]

The times clearly are disturbing. They have been a long time in the making. We didn't just wake up one morning and find the world absent of virtue. While we cannot blame one group or organization for all of society's ills, I do believe that when it comes to the negative influences facing our daughters, there is one aspect in our country's history that has negatively impacted women of all ages, including our daughters, more than any other. What is it? The Sexual Revolution.

Woman's Liberation and the Sexual Revolution

Let's turn the clocks back to the early 1960s. Think tie-dye. Think Woodstock. Think hippies. Think sexual revolution. Most of us are old enough to have at least a basic knowledge of the radical women's liberation movement that was birthed in the early 1960s.

Actually, the women's movement has been around for some time. It originated as a positive cause that evolved in the mid-1850s along with other social reform groups, including the Abolition of Slavery and the Social Purity and Temperance movements. Women began to realize that in order to transform societal ills, they needed to develop their own organizations. The original campaign included a range of issues, including the guardianship of infants, property rights, divorce, access to higher education, and equal pay. The early movement became best known for gaining the right of women to vote in 1928.

Later, during World War II, women began to enter the workforce out of necessity. In doing so, they challenged the stereotype of the traditional stay-at-home mother who was supported by her husband, the sole breadwinner. Then in the 1960s and 1970s, the women's movement took a more radical turn with the onset of "the Pill," which initiated the sexual revolution. "The Pill" allowed many women to believe they could have sex whenever they wanted, with whomever they wanted, with no strings attached. In those instances where "the Pill" didn't work, feminists demanded the right to abortion on demand.

The woman most often referred to as the founder of the radical women's liberation movement is Betty Friedan. In 1963 she published *The Feminine Mystique*, a book that stated that society puts pressures on women to be housewives and discourages them from seeking a career. In 1966 she founded the National Organization for Women (NOW).

Soon after, Gloria Steinem entered the picture. She, along with Betty Friedan and other women, published the first issue of *Ms.* magazine in 1971 and launched it as a monthly magazine in 1972. Gloria Steinem is known as a primary influence in the sexual revolution of the late 60s and early 70s. She discouraged the institution of marriage and once said, "A woman needs a man like a fish needs a bicycle." She later said, "I don't think marriage has a good name. . . . Legally speaking, it was designed for a person and a half. You became a semi-nonperson when you got married."[22] While few women were willing to shed the institution of marriage altogether at the suggestion of Ms. Steinem, many were influenced to shuck the idea of waiting until marriage to have sex.

Ironically, in 2000, Gloria Steinem wed at the age of sixty-six. Apparently she ran across a fish in need of a bicycle. For someone who influenced countless women with her radical views concerning women's rights, she apparently failed in the end to adhere to her own view against marriage. If she couldn't follow through with her own views, why should other women do so?

If Gloria Steinem proved to be an unreliable representative of a movement that influenced masses of women, what about Betty Friedan? In *Betty Friedan, Her Life*, a biography written by Judith Hennessee, the author finds it difficult to reconcile Betty Friedan, the visionary, with Betty Friedan, the woman. It turns out that the "great liberator of women" was

ill-tempered, selfish, ego-driven, arrogant, and altogether dis-
agreeable. Further, readers are told that Ms. Friedan saw no
irony in calling a meeting of feminist organizers in her New
York apartment, then employing a black maid in a white uniform to serve refreshments. Wasn't this the leader of the movement who supposedly sought equality for all women? Perhaps
most shocking is the fact that Friedan is commonly known as
"the feminist who didn't like women!"[23]

How sad that so many women have been led astray by a
movement that was led and represented by these two women.
They made up the rules as they went along, and when it
became convenient or helpful to suit their own personal preferences and agendas, they ignored or changed their rules.
Unfortunately, by the time their character flaws were exposed,
it was too late. The radical women's movement had gained
wings of its own and had taken flight.

In 1 Corinthians 3:18–19 the words of the apostle Paul
ring true of these women:

> Do not deceive yourselves. If any one of you
> thinks he is wise by the standards of this age, he
> should become a "fool" so that he may become wise.
> For the wisdom of this world is foolishness in God's
> sight. As it is written: "He catches the wise in their
> craftiness."

So why the history lesson? Is it necessary? You bet! If
we are to raise our daughters to be godly, virtuous women, we
must first understand what was primarily responsible for the
downturn in virtue among women. It is my belief that the sexual revolution, which evolved out of the radical women's liberation movement, is to blame for many of the negative
influences facing our daughters today. While an objective
Christian must admit to some merit of the women's movement—such as its justified campaign for equal pay for equal
work—overall, it has had a devastating impact on women in

our society through its campaigns for sexual freedom, abortion on demand, and self-empowerment.

Today the radical women's liberation movement, led primarily by Friedan and Steinem, seems to have died down. In the end, women were not willing to embrace the radical tenets of the movement, such as its antimarriage agenda. Women generally "discovered" that they actually do *need* men. Now, however, a new and revised version of the women's movement has begun to evolve. Waiting in the wings to take the place of the radical women's liberation movement is what is commonly referred to as "revised feminist ideology." If you think the original movement was damaging to young women, the fallout from this movement will be even more devastating. Our daughters will be hard-pressed to escape the influence of revised feminist ideology. Its message is peddled through television, movies, magazines, music, and other media outlets—making it virtually inescapable.

From Burning Bras to Push-Up Bras

What is "revised feminist ideology?" It is an offshoot of the radical women's liberation movement, minus the extremes. It is pro-career and antagonistic to stay-at-home mothers. It is sexual freedom with no strings attached. It is self-empowerment and independence. It tells girls and women to set their own rules and do whatever feels good because it's all about *them*. In general, it is a message that tells girls and women, "You can have it all!"

Let me give you an absurd, even laughable, example of revised feminist ideology that recently made its way into my inbox. It was from the popular teen fashion magazine *CosmoGIRL!* (the teen version of *Cosmopolitan*). The magazine was promoting a campaign directed at teen girls called "Girls on top." In an online teaser ad used to lure girls to participate, here is what I read:

PROJECT 2024

Our bet? In the year 2024, one *CosmoGIRL!* reader will become president of the United States. The rest of you will be CEOs, executives, and leaders. Consider this your power road map.

What's your dream? Do you want to make a million dollars by the time you're 25? You'll come home each night to your mansion and kiss your foxy husband and adorable kids hello before you rush to pack for your business trip. And hey, do they want to come with you? Why not? You're the boss! Or maybe you want to be the biggest boss of all. As in world leader. As in president of the United States. No, CosmoGIRL!—this is no fantasy. Welcome to your reality. . . .

Hmmm . . . I couldn't help but notice they didn't include the possibility that some girls may want to be *mothers*. And puhleese—a million dollars, a mansion, and a foxy husband all by the age of 25? Now, that's realistic. Heaven help us all if a CosmoGIRL! becomes president of the United States. Time to pack up and move to Canada!

It is clear that the barometer to "having it all" is achievement in the workplace. Unfortunately, this "you can have it all" message has encouraged many women to postpone marriage and/or having children in order to first establish themselves in their careers. However, a book by Sylvia Ann Hewlett entitled *Creating a Life: Professional Women and the Quest for Children* reveals that many professional women who succumbed to the message and poured themselves into building their careers, now feel ripped off and betrayed as they find themselves in their late thirties or early forties and unable to have children. The research, published in *Time* magazine, found that more than half of the thirty-five-year-old female professionals it surveyed and 42 percent of the forty-year-olds were childless. Ms. Hewlett told *Time* magazine that women are "shocked, devastated and angry."[24]

Just as the serpent deceived Eve in the garden with a quick-fix solution to "having it all," many women today have bought into the same scheme of the enemy. Rather than learn a lesson from Eve, they continue to line up to try the forbidden fruit for themselves. Mothers must be faithful in exposing their daughters to the enemy's modern-day scheme, revealing it for what it is: a lie that could leave them with power, success, and wealth but in the end—emptiness.

The main problem with revised feminist ideology is that it blatantly contradicts itself. Let me explain. One of its major tenets is that women should be independent (i.e., not be dependent on men). Another of its major tenets is that women have the right to sexual freedom. This compares to the messages sent by the radical women's movement, but it has a caveat. The revised tenet sends a message to women that basically says, "You can have sex with whomever you want, whenever you want, with no strings attached, *but* in order to get the man who will enable you to exercise your *freedom*, you must dress scantily and practice shallow 'snag-a-man' magazine tactics." (Think Monica Lewinsky here.) How ironic that the very movement that preaches women's independence from men also encourages women to be dependent on men so they can exercise their sexual freedom! (Of course, you don't hear many guys complaining.)

I am a collector of old magazines. I own quite a few *Seventeen* magazines dating back as early as 1950. It is amazing to compare the *Seventeen* magazines from the 1950s and 1960s, prior to the onset of the women's liberation movement, to *Seventeen* magazines of today. Sprinkled throughout the earlier magazines are multitudes of advertisements for Lane hope chests, engagement rings, and sterling silver flatware. In one issue from 1960, I counted ten ads for sterling silver flatware and three ads for engagement/wedding sets. One ad for silver flatware reads, "You've chosen your pattern—you've bought your first piece. It's a symbol of the home you'll have some-day."[25] Another ad reads, "Most girls start collecting Towle when they first begin to think of marriage and a home of their own, very often before they have met the man of their choice."[26] By the early 1970s, the silver flatware ads and engagement set ads had dwindled to an average of one ad per issue.[27]

Compare those advertisements to advertisements in current *Seventeen* magazines. In place of the ads for silver flatware, engagement sets, and hope chests are ads for makeup, hair care products, and raunchy clothing lines. One ad for a popular teen fashion line shows a girl waiting in line for a concert with a very bare midriff and the strap of her thong underwear coming out the top of her low-rider jeans. Tucked inside the strap of her thong underwear is her concert ticket. A girl behind her, who is holding her ticket in her hand, is clearly miffed as a handsome boy unlatches a velvet rope and allows the young lady with the precariously placed concert ticket early entrance to the show. Another provocative ad shows a scantily dressed girl lying in the backseat of a car with her knees apart and a sultry "come hither" look on her face. Both ads send a clear message that when you dress to please the opposite sex, you are guaranteed attention from the guys, albeit in the backseat of a car.

In the older *Seventeen* magazines, there were a few ads and articles that centered on pleasing the opposite sex, but they focused on the actual product rather than sexuality. Most of the ads or articles peddled products such as deodorant, hand lotion, or food. One of my all-time favorite "snag-a-man" articles had the title, "Make him a pie!"[28] Another *Seventeen* had an ad that said, "Beats Going Out! A Chef Boy-Ar-Dee pizza convinces boys there's no place like home as no store-bought pizza can."[29] Yet another ad said, "Good date idea. . . . Feed him delicious Date Corn Bread—and he can easily see how nice you are!"[30] I must remember to share that one with my daughter when she is of dating age. The girls in these ads opted for an apron to lure their man rather than cleavage-baring blouses and thong underwear. The ads clearly were based on the old adage that "the way to a man's heart is through his stomach."

From the Age of Innocence to the Age of Seduction

Perhaps the most shocking contrast between then and now is found in the magazines' featured short stories geared to teen girls. In the December 1948 *Ladies' Home Journal*, the featured short story is titled "Security," and the caption reads: "She said brokenly, 'I don't want to wait.' Her eyes were closed, the lashes sooty against her skin." Sound racy? Don't get the wrong idea. Read on and you discover the main character is referring to waiting, of all things, to get married. Her father believes a man should hold a steady job before getting married and has forbidden marriage until the lad can find a steady and secure job. In the end, the couple respectfully abides by the wishes of the father.[31]

Compare this to the featured short story in the December 2001 *Seventeen* magazine, titled "Seduce Me." The caption below the title reads: "Mom's dead. Dad's dating Sylvia. What's to stop me from sleeping with Sylvia's son?" The main character is a sixteen-year-old girl. In one part of the story, her best friend quips, "At least your father's getting laid. That's more than we can say for ourselves." Later in the story, when the main character is alone with Sylvia's son, it reads, "He locked the door with a loud click. Maybe he'd seduce me right there on the couch. The next day I'd be queen of the lunchroom, telling my friends what it was like to no longer be a virgin." Her wishes are not fulfilled, and she later tells her best friend, "My dad's living the life of Fabio, and I'm going to die a miserable virgin."[32]

How unfortunate that *Seventeen* has a large platform to influence preteen and teen girls in a positive way, yet their inclusion of stories such as this sends a clear message to girls that they are abnormal freaks if they remain virgins. If the publishers of these types of magazines sincerely care about their target audience, perhaps they would focus on the fact that 72 percent of teen girls regret their decision to have sex and wish they had waited.[33] They would also educate their audience to the dangers of sex outside of marriage, including sexually transmitted diseases, AIDS, and unwanted pregnancies.

In a 1948 issue of *Ladies' Home Journal*, there is an advice column answered by none other than Eleanor Roosevelt. One young woman submitted this question: "What is the reason men of the North seemingly show lack of respect for women? Men do not tip their hats to women whom they meet on the street, neither do they rise from their seats when women come into the room. Southern men are more courteous." Mrs. Roosevelt replied, "You surprise me in your estimate of men in the North. I have never had a man greet me in the street without raising his hat, nor do I find that they do not get up when a lady comes into the room."[34]

Mrs. Roosevelt would roll over in her grave if she could see the "progress" women have made.

We have the women's liberation movement to thank for the fact that few men open doors for women and surrender their seats to women. Women have been taught that they are far too independent for that. For heaven's sakes, we wouldn't want men to *respect* us, would we? Besides, why bother with that kind of respect when women can get respect for so much more—like plunging necklines, bare midriffs, and painted-on jeans. Now that's progress! In times long past, men had to pay a cover charge to see women dressed like that. I must remember to pen a thank-you note to Ms. Friedan and Ms. Steinem for spearheading a movement that has redefined *respect* when it comes to the opposite sex.

Other Media Influences

While I have focused primarily on the medium of teen and women's fashion magazines as the conduit for revised feminist ideology, let's not forget that the message is also peddled through television, movies, music, and other media influences. My husband recalls being teased as a teenager because his mother would not allow him to watch the popular sitcom *Happy Days* (because Fonzie was a hood). My, how times have changed. The racy sitcoms of today make *Happy Days* look more like a *Barney* rerun.

We have since graduated to many sitcoms with professional career women who, oftentimes, show up to work in miniskirts, talk crassly, and come on to the men in their office. In addition, the "professional" female characters are often portrayed as being confused, emotionally conflicted, and flighty. Was this what the women's movement had in mind when it talked about breaking the glass ceiling in the workplace? I'd rather peddle Kirby vacuums door-to-door than work with someone as flaky as Ally McBeal!

Movies similarly portray women in a negative manner. It's no secret that R-rated movies are marketed directly to teens, in spite of the fact that most teens are younger than seventeen. If the movie is geared to teens, you can almost be assured that the female characters will not be portrayed in a positive, respectful manner. The pop music of the day is no different. It is full of suggestive, gratuitous, and often degrading lyrics about women. Thanks to Britney Spears, J-Lo, and other pop divas, our daughters not only want to sing the risqué lyrics; they want to dress the part as well.

The message of revised feminist ideology is clear: You can have it all! You set the rules. Unless, of course, you want a man, and then you have to play by *his* rules. Taunt him. Tease him. Give him what he wants—all in the name of sexual freedom. The sad thing is that this is not what girls *want*. I talk to countless Christian teen girls, college women, and women who have unknowingly bought into the messages of the revised feminist ideology. They feel empty, used, shameful, and directionless.

> They soon forgot His works; they did not wait
> for His counsel,
> But lusted exceedingly in the wilderness, and
> tested God in the desert.
> And He gave them their request, but sent lean-
> ness into their soul. (Ps. 106:13–15 NKJV)

My Story

You might wonder how I know so much about the women's movement. Unfortunately, I learned most of it the hard way. I am one of the many victims who bought into the teachings of the movement hook, line, and sinker. By the time I got to college, I was a self-professed agnostic feminist. Gloria Steinem was my hero. I recall attending a NOW meeting on the University of Texas campus and coming away confused. The girls I met at the meeting were radical feminists who were haters of men. I considered myself a feminist, but I didn't hate men. I wasn't a match for NOW, but I was a perfect fit for the revised feminist ideology that was beginning to take root and sweep the country. There was no formal group to join, and like most other girls my age, I wasn't even aware there was a name for the movement to which I had succumbed. The fallout was immense. In my junior year I found myself guilt-ridden, confused, and most of all, empty. In the midst of these feelings, a friend invited me to attend a Christian retreat for college students over Labor Day weekend. I accepted the invitation.

The first evening at the retreat, a speaker shared how he had previously had a void in his heart. He had attempted to fill the void with everything the world had to offer. As he shared about the emptiness that followed, I began to fidget uncomfortably in my chair. His story hit too close to home.

He shared how he had been at the end of his
friend had taken the time to share with him abou.. ... .
ditional love of God. He talked about how God proved His
love by sending His Son, Jesus Christ, to die on a cross. But
what spoke to my heart more than anything was when he
shared that only Jesus Christ could fill the void and emptiness in our hearts. He concluded by inviting each person to
accept Christ as his or her Lord and Savior, as he had done
earlier in his life.

When he finished, the worship leader led us in a chorus.
As I was singing, I felt my hardened heart begin to soften.
A million thoughts were racing through my mind: *Could he be
right? Could this Jesus fill the void in my heart? Is my search for
happiness and fulfillment over?* As I stood there arguing silently
back and forth with myself, I finally gave up. On about the
eleventh chorus of "I Have Decided to Follow Jesus" (a dead
giveaway it was a Baptist-sponsored event), I gave my heart to
Christ. The void in my heart was finally filled, and my life has
never been the same since.

What about You?

Many of us have been conned by a movement that has failed
to define or justify itself over the years. The original women's
movement of the 1960s and 1970s had women burning their
bras in the streets and throwing out their razors. The revised
version of today has women wearing push-up bras and scoop
neck T-shirts and doing whatever it takes to make men drool.
One can only imagine what is next. If we are to adequately
counteract the movement's impact on our daughters, we must
warn them that the movement will dangle before their eyes a
carrot called "happiness and fulfillment." In the end, however,
it will leave many empty and broken hearts in its wake. As
Christian mothers, we must awaken from our slumber, equip
ourselves for battle, and refuse to allow the world to take our
girls by the hand and lead them through life. If we don't take

action, be assured, our daughters will be indoctrinated into the popular thinking of the day.

Needless to say, I will not be surprising my daughter with a subscription to *Seventeen* magazine in her stocking this Christmas. My daughter will be taught that everyone has a huge, gaping hole within their heart that can only be satisfied by the perfect love of Jesus Christ. She will be reminded that Jesus liberated all women more than two thousand years ago when He died on the cross for our sins. His movement never has been and never will be quenched as it continues to spread to every corner of the world. As a leader, Jesus is credible, reliable, and has a glowing list of references that attest to His life-changing power. He doesn't change the rules to match the times. He is the same yesterday, today, and forever. My daughter will be encouraged to keep these truths in mind as she encounters other young ladies who have fallen prey to the negative influences of the culture and have attempted to fill the huge holes in their hearts with anything but the unfailing love of God. Wow, it almost sounds as if I am suggesting that Christian women need to start a *new* women's movement.

Jeremiah 6:16 says, "Stand at the crossroads and look; ask for the ancient paths, ask where the good way is, and walk in it, and you will find rest for your souls." Our girls are in desperate need of new direction. The women's movement has failed them. Our culture has failed them. They long for rest in their souls. We have the answer. We know the good way. It's time for a new women's movement. For the sake of our daughters, let's not rest until we see it happen. John 8:36 says it best:

"So if the Son sets you free, you will be free indeed."

I have lived nearly sixty years with myself and
my own century and am not so enamored of either
as to desire no glimpse of a world beyond them.
—C. S. Lewis

Questions for Individual Reflection or Group Study

1. What statistics listed on pages 6–7 did you find most shocking? Why?

2. How have you personally been affected by the lies and negative messages of the women's movement? (sexual freedom, the message of "you can have it all," anti-family, etc.)

3. In what way(s) could you relate to my story? Have you been "liberated" by Jesus Christ? Think back on the day you were liberated and thank Jesus for your freedom.

4. Have you or your daughter been affected by revised feminist ideology? If so, how?

5. What worries you most when it comes to raising your daughter to be a godly woman?

CHAPTER TWO

Motherhood:
A High Calling

*I*t is my conviction that many mothers will occupy a higher position in God's kingdom than many prominent Christian leaders whom we might expect to find in places of greater honor.

Think of some of the great men of the Bible like Moses, Samuel, and Timothy. Where would they have been had it not been for their praying, Spirit-led mothers? Think of Augustine, John Newton, and the zealous Wesleys; their names may never have lighted the pages of history had it not been for the blessed influence of godly mothers!

The simple prayers from our infant lips were but echoes from our mother's heart. Can we ever forget the soft caresses of those hands of blessing on our heads as we knelt by our beds? Can we fail to remember her night vigils, her seasons of intercession, her well-marked Bible, and her words of admonition? Her actions spoke eloquently of Him who taught us of the greater love of God.

> What a tragedy to neglect the counsel of a godly
> mother! What eternal consequences to reject her
> God . . . "Do not forsake the law of your mother"
> (Prov. 1:8). —Henry G. Bosch[1]

President John Quincy Adams once said, "From all that
I had read of history and government of human life and manners, I had drawn this conclusion, that the manners of women
were the most infallible barometer to ascertain the degree of
morality and virtue of a nation."[2]

This is certainly a humbling thought, given the current
absence of virtue in our culture. Yet, rather than resolve ourselves to the times with an attitude that says, "It's too little too
late," I suggest we rise up to the challenge and give it everything we've got. If President Adams is right and the manners of
women have a direct impact on the morality and virtue of a
nation, then as mothers of daughters, we have received a high
calling.

In chapter 1, we looked at the current times and the negative impact the sexual revolution has had on our culture. In
this chapter we will examine the tremendous calling God has
placed on our lives as mothers to impact the next generation
of women, starting with our daughters. In a culture that
esteems success, wealth, knowledge, and power for women,
motherhood fails even to make the ballot when it comes to
noteworthy aspirations. This is in spite of the fact that no
greater influence exists than that of a mother to her child. If
we are to raise godly seed for the next generation, we must
devote ourselves to this high calling with purpose and determination. We cannot abdicate the spiritual training of our children to the local church, a private Christian school, or any
other well-meaning organization.

In a 2002 nationwide survey that was conducted by
George Barna (the renown pollster), a random sampling of
more than one thousand adults were asked a question regarding the collapse of Enron, WorldCom and other companies.

Participants were asked what, in their opinion, would have helped avoid these problems completely, mostly, only a little, or not at all. They were given six choices from which to choose. The majority (72 percent) of the people polled agreed that the problems could have been "completely" or "mostly" avoided had "parents spent more time teaching their children appropriate values." This topped such choices as "business executives had better training in ethics," "government regulations were more demanding," and "American society had a stronger moral foundation."[3] The poll reveals that even the public at large recognizes the powerful influence parents can have in shaping the value systems of their children—a value system that will be carried into their families, workplaces, and communities.

Parenting a child has always been a challenging task, but never more difficult than today. Our grandparents and, for the most part, our parents had the privilege of raising their children in a culture that was friendly to the Judeo-Christian value system upon which our nation was founded. Today, however, we find ourselves swimming upstream in a culture that is tolerant of everything *but* Christianity. Essentially, God has been removed from the workplace, public schools, and government.

How could this have happened when, even today, 84 percent of Americans claim to believe that Jesus Christ is God or the Son of God, and 61 percent say religion can solve all or most of today's problems.[4] If this is true, Christians are clearly the majority in America. Why are we so strangely silent? If we are to save our children from the tight grip of postmodern culture, we must be willing to speak up and say, "Enough!" We must recognize the power and responsibility we have been given as mothers to shape an entire generation.

George Barna recently said, "More than many people want to admit, how we train our children determines their values, views and behaviors as adults. If you want a moral society, you must develop it by raising children who understand and embrace good values and standards."[5]

In part 2, we will look at six battles that we, as mothers, should choose to fight if we are to counteract the culture and raise our daughters to be the godly, virtuous young women God intends. Before doing so, however, it is necessary that we first put our call as mothers into the proper perspective.

A Noble Profession

There is nothing quite like being a mother. The hours can be long and exhausting, but the payoff is immense. Wide is the gamut of emotions in motherhood. One minute you can be lauding the virtues of motherhood, and the next minute you're screaming, "Calgon, take me away . . . or better yet, take them away!"

It would be easy to view motherhood as a low-ranking job, given the limited attention it receives in our society. I'll admit it was hard for me to view motherhood as a worthy call after being thoroughly brainwashed by revised feminist ideology. Early on as a new mother, I would often compare myself to other mothers who seemed to have it all together. You know, the ones with tidy houses, brownies in the oven, and scrapbooks documenting every minute of their children's lives. Try as I may, I just couldn't measure up. I eventually came to the conclusion that it would be far better for my children to have a domestically challenged mother than a spiritually challenged mother. Bless my kids' hearts, I'll even throw in a few shoe boxes of their childhood pictures when they leave the nest.

Motherhood can be a daunting task. Many studies reveal that the most formative years of a child's life are their earliest years. It is clear that mothers have a tremendous influence on their children when they are young. What child doesn't adore his/her mother when he/she is young? I remember when my son, Ryan, was a toddler and he would tell me, "Mom, when I grow up, I'm going to marry you." Now, in high school, this same child instructs me to walk ten paces behind him in public, lest anyone see him out with his *mother* and mistake him for a mama's boy.

But here's a newsflash to mothers who wonder if the prime years of influence end with the onset of the teen years: George Barna, in his book *Real Teens*, says, "Although millions of mothers of teens would faint at the idea, Mom is typically the most revered figure in the life of a teenager." Get out the smelling salts. Personally, this mother is shocked, but encouraged. Further, when Barna surveyed teens and asked what grade they would give Mom for her parenting prowess, three-quarters gave her an A, one-fifth awarded her a B and just 6 percent gave their mothers a C or lower.[6] Clearly, teens are watching, listening (even if they roll their eyes), and looking for direction.

I find it interesting that in 2 Kings, when the reign of a new king was introduced, the name of his mother was often included. With each king we are told that he either "did what was good in the eyes of the LORD" or "did what was evil in the eyes of the LORD." Can you imagine if we were to look over our respective family trees and find listed beside the name of each deceased relative one of those two phrases—"did what was good in the eyes of the LORD" or "did what was evil in the eyes of the LORD?" Further, what if we were to find the name of each relative's mother listed directly beside the phrase? I am certainly not suggesting that mothers are to blame if their grown children choose not to walk in the ways of the Lord. I have known plenty of godly mothers who were devoted to the spiritual training of their children only to experience the heartbreak of one or more of the children becoming prodigals. Our children will ultimately make their own decisions regarding matters of faith. Still, regardless of what they choose (good or evil), a mother will forever be linked to her child.

Help Wanted

One of the first phrases my daughter uttered was, "I do it myself." I was hoping for "Mommy, I love you," but instead I got "I do it myself." When she was two, I found the little pixie standing on the kitchen counter getting a cup down. When I winced, she looked at me and said, "I do it myself." When she was four, I found her in her room hammering a nail into the wall to hang a picture. Unfortunately, she used a thick roofing nail. All was forgiven when she cocked her curly blonde head and said, "I do it myself."

Initially, I admired her independence and can-do spirit. However, I know firsthand the dangers of an "I do it myself" attitude when it comes to a relationship with God. Those of us who have "I do it myself" attitudes often have a hard time asking God for help. When it comes to mothering, it is impossible to "do it ourselves." The best mothers are those who admit that the job is far too big to handle alone. They lay their inadequacies at the foot of the cross and rush to His throne for advice. When their children stray from the path, as they often will, faithful mothers cry out to the Lord in groanings too deep for words. They trust God to draw their children's wayward hearts back to His paths. He is, after all, their Creator.

One of the most beautiful accounts of maternal love found in Scripture is the account of Hannah in 1 Samuel 1:11–28. Barren for many years, Hannah cried out to God for a son and vowed to give him over to God, should God comply by meeting her request. God blessed her with a son, Samuel; and true to her word, she cared for him until he was weaned, then brought him to Eli, the priest, to live out the remainder of his childhood years at the temple.

> After he was weaned, she took the boy with her, young as he was, along with a three-year-old bull, an ephah of flour and a skin of wine, and brought him to the house of the LORD at Shiloh. When they had slaughtered the bull, they brought the boy to Eli, and she said to him, "As surely as you live, my lord, I am the woman who stood here beside you praying to the LORD. I prayed for this child, and the LORD has

granted me what I asked of him. So now I give him
to the LORD. For his whole life he will be given over
to the LORD." And he worshiped the LORD there.
(1 Sam. 1:24–28)

What mother could take a child she had nursed at her
breast, swayed to sleep in her arms, and watched take his first
wobbly steps and put him in the care of a stranger for the
remainder of his childhood years? Only a woman desperately
dependent on God. Hannah was able to follow through with
her vow to commit her son to the care of the Lord because she
had come to desperately depend on God prior to Samuel's
birth. When Hannah was barren, we are told that she "poured
out" her soul to the Lord (1 Sam. 1:15). The original Hebrew
word used for "poured out" is *shaphak*, which means to "spill
forth" or "sprawl out." Hannah was in the habit of depending
on God long before she had children. Vow or no vow, Hannah
knew better than to think Samuel belonged to her.

After turning Samuel over to the priest Eli, the next verse
gives us great insight into Hannah's walk with God: "Then
Hannah prayed and said: 'My heart rejoices in the LORD'"
(1 Sam. 2:1). I'd be curled up in a fetal position sobbing my
eyes out, but Hannah rejoiced! Dear mothers, let us pay close
heed to Hannah's example. Our children belong first and foremost to the Lord. He has entrusted each of them into our care
for a short time.

Even though Samuel was given over to the Lord, he was
not exempt from ungodly influences while in the care of Eli.
Scripture tells us that Eli's sons were guilty of treating the
Lord's offerings, which had been brought by the Israelites, with
contempt; they also were sleeping with the women who served
at the entrance of the Tent of Meeting. Ironically, Samuel was
the one who eventually delivered the Lord's spoken judgment
against the house of Eli.

As my children have gotten older and have been exposed
to ungodly influences outside of my care and control, I have had

to mentally turn them over to the Lord as an act of my will. I cannot watch them every minute of every day, but God can.

Often, when I tuck my children in at night and say bedtime prayers, I thank God for choosing me to be the mother of His precious children. I say this aloud because I want to make sure they understand the order of the hierarchy, lest they mistakenly think their father and I are at the top. We answer to God and are accountable to Him for the care and training they receive. What an awesome thought that God has entrusted His children into our care for a short time. We have eighteen years to equip our children to live in the real world. We have eighteen years to introduce our children to the one true God and encourage them to claim Him for their very own. We have eighteen years to raise our children to "do what is good in the eyes of the LORD." It certainly puts a new perspective on the high calling of parenting, and more specifically, motherhood.

Walk the Talk and Talk the Walk

In Deuteronomy 6:4–9, Moses exhorted the Israelites with the following challenge concerning their responsibility as parents:

> Hear, O Israel: The LORD our God, the LORD is one. Love the LORD your God with all your heart and with all your soul and with all your strength. These commandments that I give you today are to be upon your hearts. Impress them on your children. Talk about them when you sit at home and when you walk along the road, when you lie down and when you get up. Tie them as symbols on your hands and bind them on your foreheads. Write them on the doorframes of your houses and on your gates.

God expects the same of parents today. He is much more concerned that our children receive proper training in His truths and principles than a coveted spot on the A team, their name on the honor roll, or even a college degree. While these things are worthy, they should not be our primary focus.

Nowadays it is more important than ever that parents are purposeful about the spiritual training of their children. It is not enough to take them to church, put them in Christian schools, and say bedtime prayers. As mothers appointed by God to raise His children in today's world, we must set forth with purpose and determination. We must have a clear understanding of God's truths in order to impress them on the hearts of our children. Impressing God's truths on our children involves teaching them with our words and showing them with our actions. In other words, we must practice what we preach and preach what we practice.

According to a Purdue University study that examined how parents influenced the religious beliefs of students ages eighteen to twenty-five, it is not enough for parents to model their beliefs to their children. If they want their children to adopt their religious beliefs, "parents have to talk about those beliefs. They have to share their thoughts with their child," says Lynn Okagaki,[7] the author of the study. She found that children were more likely to adopt their parent's beliefs when they had a clear understanding of what their parents believed.

If we are to counteract the negative influences of the culture, we must be armed with God's truths and teach them to our children. We must talk about God's truths when we sit at home and when we walk along the road, when we lie down and when we get up. And we must do so in the hearing of our children. A mother's commitment to pass down God's truths to her children can literally impact the souls of future grand-children and great-grandchildren for generations to come. As mothers of daughters who are exposed to the negative influences of revised feminist ideology and secular humanism run amuck, we face a challenge that, at times, seems insurmountable. Yet be reminded, we are not alone. God has equipped us with everything we need to accomplish His purposes. In part 2, we will discuss in more detail what we, as mothers, can do to counteract the negative influences of the culture and raise our daughters to be godly.

Excuses, Excuses

Why then would a Christian mother neglect her responsibility to impart God's truths to her daughters? Following are four common reasons.

1. "I'm too busy"

If your schedule is anything like mine, you meet yourself coming and going. I have days where I call out spelling words at stoplights on the way to pick up my third carpool of the day. I spritz perfume on the cheerleading uniform that I ran out of time to wash in my haste to whip up a last-minute costume for the Greco-Roman feast at school. I am the mother screaming "Hallelujah! Praise God for skillet dinners!" on the frozen food aisle at 5 p.m. Before I know it, the day is over. I collapse into my bed, only to awaken the next morning and start all over.

Busyness is a way of life, but the truth is, we make time for the things we deem to be important. I cannot imagine anything more important than the spiritual training of our daughters. No doubt, the fruits of team sports, piano lessons, and a good education will benefit our daughters for years to come. However, training them to walk in God's ways will impact them for *eternity*.

My husband and I have had to say no to our children's requests to participate in some activities that in a vacuum may be worthy in themselves, but had we said yes, would have produced such a frenzied pace that our time for spiritual training would have been inhibited. By the time I drop my children off at college, I want to know that, as their mother, I gave it my best effort when it came to their spiritual training. This is especially important given the fact that 30 percent to 51 percent of Christian college students renounce their faith before graduating from college.[8]

2. "I want to be her friend"

Deep down inside every mother wants her daughter to *like* her. This natural inclination gets out of balance, however, if the mother cares more about being her daughter's hip and cool friend than she does about being her mother. Sometimes this occurs because the mother has a deep need for acceptance. It also may be rooted in a desire to have a closer mother-daughter relationship than the mother was able to have with her own mother. Regardless, a mother who is more concerned about being a "friend" first and a "mom" second, does her daughter a great disservice. Though it is a natural desire to want to be loved by others, especially our children, Jesus put the matter into perspective when He said, "Anyone who loves his father or mother more than me is not worthy of me; anyone who loves his son or daughter more than me is not worthy of me" (Matt. 10:37).

It is possible to be both "mom" and "friend," but it is a fine balancing act. My daughter and I have a wonderful relationship. Just recently I checked her online profile under her instant-messaging screen name. Most kids who send instant messages to their friends have profiles they have created about themselves. The profiles often include "shout-outs" to their friends. (I know I've lost many of you "nontechie" moms, but bear with me. We will discuss the influence of the Internet in the next chapter, so you will be well versed in basic Internet teen vocabulary.) "Shout-outs" are memories and inside jokes between you and the person to whom you have directed your shout-out. I was amazed to find that my sweet daughter had included me in her shout-outs. Here is what it said:

> Mommy—mighty morphin mother; cheetah;
> dancin' in the dentist office; shake your groove
> thing . . . show 'em how to do it, yah; Mrs. Hawiggins;
> Louie Lobster; weeping, weeping; normal mother;
> running into signs at the mall; fluffy index . . . I love
> you, Mom! Thanks so much for everything! BFF
> [best friends forever]

Of course, I knew the meaning behind every cryptic word of her shout-out. Everything she had written represented a past memory that bonds us together. As I read her shout-out, I was moved to tears. I don't know of many middle-school girls who admit to liking their mothers *and* back it up in writing. I do not claim to be an authority on mother-daughter relationships, but I can tell you that I have worked very hard at being first her mother and then her friend. We have fun together, but I also draw a firm line in the sand when it comes to negative influences that would compromise the spiritual training of my daughter. Trust me, it may not be the "cool" thing to do, but it is the right thing to do. I realize that there will most likely come a day when my stand for what is true and right may leave my daughter striking me from her online profile and throwing darts at my picture in her room. I hope it doesn't come to that, but if it does, I will persevere in my high calling. Besides, we all know what happens when they have children of their own. . . .

3. "I am not that knowledgeable when it comes to the Bible and teaching God's truths"

Another common reason a mother may neglect her responsibility to impart God's truths to her daughter is a lack of spiritual knowledge regarding God's truths. Just as we will make time for the things that are important to us, we will also obtain knowledge in areas we deem to be important. My family was recently in the market for a puppy. Considering the fact that this little critter would be a part of our lives for an average of twelve to sixteen years, I poured myself into researching the pros and cons of a multitude of breeds. If only I had been as committed to my studies in college! I am now a walking dog encyclopedia. The fruits of my labor paid off, and we are the proud owners of a Yorkshire "Terror." (No, in case you are wondering, that is not a typo.) No fault of her own, she is a product of her environment. My daughter coddles her and dresses her up in doll clothes. My sons wrestle with her and have taught her to attack on command. She is a four-pound furball suffering from multiple personality disorder.

When it comes to spiritual truths, I have always been able to verbalize *what* I believe since becoming a Christian, but I was lacking in my ability to explain *why* I believe it. As I began to realize the importance of defending my faith to others, I poured myself into researching the concept of a Christian worldview. Believe me, I am not a good student by nature. My husband is the brain-o in this family. He graduated valedictorian of chemical engineering at the University of Texas with a 3.96 GPA. He made only two Bs during his four years of college. In fact, we had that in common—only I was rather excited about my two Bs! Trust me, if I can become knowl-edgeable about God's truths, so can you. I have become a faith-ful and devoted student. I have hit the books—or rather, the Good Book. I am driven by the frightening realization that my ability to verbalize effectively what I believe and why I believe it will impact generations to come on the Courtney family tree.

4. "The world is not all that bad"

Denial or apathy concerning the times is another common reason mothers may neglect the spiritual training of their daughters. If after reading chapter 1 you still find yourself mumbling, "The world is not all that bad," I have a *sweet* little Yorkie puppy I want to sell you. Don't be fooled; there's a bat-tle going on out there. The truth is, as Christians, we should have acted sooner to counteract the negative influences in our culture. I've heard it said that the best time to plant a tree was ten years ago; the second best time is *now*. Let's not miss this opportunity to act.

God has bestowed upon each of us the honorary title of "mother." I can imagine no greater blessing than to raise my children to "do good in the eyes of the LORD," so they can, in turn, raise their children to "do good in the eyes of the LORD," and so on and so on and so on. The very souls of our children, grandchildren, and great grandchildren are at stake. The times are serious, and it's time to get serious. As mothers, we must unite, take up our weapons, and stand for Truth. We have been called for such a time as this. It's time to prepare for battle.

Questions for Individual Reflection or Group Study

1. Do you agree or disagree with John Adam's quote in which he linked the manners of women to the virtue and morality of a nation? Why or why not?

2. In your opinion, do you feel that Christians are the "silent majority" when it comes to influencing the times? Why or why not?

3. Have you given your daughter over to the Lord and acknowledged that she belongs to Him first and foremost?

4. Is it currently a priority in your life to pass down God's truths to your daughter? If not, could you relate to any of the four reasons (excuses) listed? Which one(s)?

CHAPTER THREE

Counteracting the Culture

*I*f chapter 1 left you mumbling, "Jesus come quickly," then hopefully, chapter 2 left you basking in the glow of the high calling of motherhood. This current chapter will continue to encourage you in your high calling as we begin to look at some solutions to counteracting the negative influences affecting our daughters. While our first inclination might be to revert to the innocent days of poodle skirts, penny loafers, and dates to the malt shop, unfortunately, this is not a realistic approach. As mothers, we must accept the reality of the current times and live in today's world, all the while doing what we can to influence tomorrow. Besides, to escape from the negative influences altogether, we would have to trade in our cars for a buggy and relocate to the nearest Amish community. Not a realistic solution for this ol' city gal. One week of getting up with the chickens and sewing my own clothes would have me scheduling an appointment with ye old Amish therapist.

While the times have certainly changed, rest confident in the assurance that our God has not changed. How comforting to know that "Jesus Christ is the same yesterday and today and forever" (Heb. 13:8). The current plight we face regarding the times is no different from Old Testament times when the

Israelite people would succumb to the negative influences of the times and find themselves empty and lacking direction. In Malachi 3:7, God said, "'Ever since the time of your forefathers you have turned away from my decrees and have not kept them. Return to me, and I will return to you,' says the LORD Almighty. 'But you ask, "How are we to return?"'" While we may not be able to turn back the clock and *return* to the days of innocence, we can, however, *return* to God. Not unlike the Israelites, we too might ask, "How are we to return?"

King Josiah

Last chapter, I spoke of the succession of kings that ruled over the Israelites. The majority left a legacy of doing "what was evil in the eyes of the LORD." Occasionally, a king would come along and buck the negative trend by doing "what was right in the eyes of the LORD." One king in particular, King Josiah, was especially commendable. Josiah became king at the young age of eight years old. Second Kings 22:2 notes that "he did what was right in the eyes of the LORD . . . not turning aside to the right or the left." Now, I don't know if you've been around a typical bunch of eight-year-old boys lately, but doing "what is right in the eyes of the LORD" does not come naturally, unless Mom is threatening to withdraw Nintendo privileges. In fact, the typical résumé of the average eight-year-old boy might include such noteworthy achievements as the ability to belch to the tune of many songs, completely ruin six new pairs of socks in a two-week period, and make a fort in the backyard that includes cacti from the neighbor's expensive zero-landscape yard. How do I know this? My son, Hayden, is nine years old, and he personally pulled off each of the above feats at the age of eight. Definitely not "king" material.

Lest you jump to conclusions and assume that Josiah did "what was right in the eyes of the LORD," because he was the product of a long line of ancestors steeped in godly heritage, let me assure you that this was not the case. His father and grandfather had enough dysfunction to make the average guest on *The Jerry Springer Show* look normal. His father, King Amon, did what was "evil in the eyes of the LORD" (2 Kings 21:20), reigned only two years, and was conspired against by his own officials and assassinated in the palace. His grandfather, King Manasseh, did what was "evil in the sight of the LORD" (2 Kings 21:2), reigned fifty-five years, and "shed so much innocent blood that he filled Jerusalem from end to end" (2 Kings 21:16). He erected altars to Baal, bowed down and worshipped the starry hosts, sacrificed his son in the fire, practiced sorcery and divination, and consulted mediums and spiritists. Not exactly a positive role model for his grandson, Josiah.

I can't help but wonder if Josiah did what was "right in the eyes of the LORD," because he had a mother who was committed to raising her children to do what was "right in the eyes of the LORD." Call it speculation, but someone was steering the boy in the right direction.

In the eighth year of Josiah's reign, when he was approximately sixteen years old, Scripture notes that Josiah began to "seek the God of his ancestor David." In the twelfth year of his reign, at approximately twenty years old, he began to "purify Judah and Jerusalem, destroying all the pagan shrines, the Asherah poles, and the carved idols and cast images" (2 Chron. 34:3 NLT).

Perhaps the most defining moment for Josiah came six years later, in the eighteenth year of his reign. After purifying the land and the temple, Josiah ordered that repairs begin on the "temple of the LORD his God" (2 Chron. 34:8). One day he sent his secretary, Shaphan, to the temple to inform Hilkiah, the high priest, to pay out the workers who were repairing the temple. While performing this task, Hilkiah informed Shaphan that he had found the Book of the Law in the temple of the Lord. Shaphan returned with the book and read from it in the presence of the king. Keep in mind that up until this point, Josiah had no knowledge of the book; he is hearing its contents for the first time. When the book was read, Josiah was faced with the sudden realization that God had previously established a covenant with the Israelite people and had set forth a code of conduct for the people to follow. Upon hearing the contents of the book and coming to terms with the shortfall of the Israelite people in meeting God's terms, Josiah humbled himself, tore his robes, and wept in the presence of the Lord (see 2 Kings 22:19).

Josiah's response to the reading of the Book of the Law and his subsequent decision to return to the teachings of the Lord can serve as a model to Christian mothers today who are faced with raising their daughters in an ungodly world. Josiah was faced with the same question the Israelites asked God in Malachi 3:7: "How are we to return?" Josiah's response ultimately led the Israelite people back to the paths of God. As we look at his response in more detail, take note as to how Josiah was able to counteract the negative influences of the times and return to God.

1. Josiah Cried Out to God and Wept in His Presence

In spite of the fact that Josiah had sought the God of his ancestor David ten years prior, purified the land six years prior, and recently had begun repairs to the temple, it became clear with the reading of the Book of the Law that the Israelite people had a long way to go in returning to the paths of God. As mothers, we face a similar situation today in raising godly, virtuous daughters. If reading the sad statistics in chapter 1 concerning our current times didn't bring tears to your eyes, I don't know what will. As someone who has been in the trenches of ministry to preteen and teen girls, I have witnessed firsthand the consequences of a culture absent of virtue and the effect it is having on the younger generation. The ministry I started several years ago for preteen and teen girls sponsors mother-daughter events throughout the country. At each event we offer separate "question and answer" (Q&A) times for middle school girls, high school girls, and mothers. In each Q&A time, attendees are given the opportunity to anonymously submit questions to be answered by a panel of qualified godly women. The questions the girls turn in are enough to put you on mascara alert. Many are too provocative to read aloud. Our worldly culture is exposing our girls to situations they are not equipped to handle. They are being forced to grow up too fast.

Like Josiah, we mothers must acknowledge the evil times and cry out to God for help. As Christians, we find ourselves in a sad and desperate state when it comes to the godless influences of our culture. Though Christians are the majority in this country, I fear that many have become apathetic concerning the times and many more appear to have adopted an attitude that says, "If you can't beat 'em, join 'em." Over the last several decades, Christians have become more and more desensitized to our worldly culture. Like the church of Laodicea mentioned in the prophetic book of Revelation, many Christians are left with a lukewarm faith that is neither "cold nor hot" (Rev. 3:15).

When we mothers humble ourselves before God and weep before Him, crying out for direction, God will have mercy and hear our prayers. If you have never been able to weep in the presence of God over the evil in this world, make a point to ask God specifically in your prayer time to break your heart. Like Josiah, our first step is to turn to God for solutions.

> If my people, who are called by my name, will humble themselves and pray and seek my face and turn from their wicked ways, then will I hear from heaven and will forgive their sin and will heal their land. (2 Chron. 7:14)

2. Josiah Pledged Himself to the Covenant

The second step Josiah took after discovering the Book of the Law was to gather the people together, from the least to the greatest, and read the entire Book of the Covenant in the hearing of the people. After doing so, he set an example before the people by making a personal pledge before God to whole-heartedly follow the commands set forth in the book: "The king stood by the pillar and renewed the covenant in the pres-ence of the LORD—to follow the LORD and keep his com-mands, regulations and decrees with all his heart and all his soul, thus confirming the words of the covenant written in this book. Then all the people pledged themselves to the covenant" (2 Kings 23:3).

When Christ came, he established a new covenant that set man free from the penalty of the law and instead promised sal-vation by grace to those who believed on His name. However, it was never God's intent that man ignore the code of conduct He had prescribed. The Bible, combining both the old and new covenants, was intended to be man's guidebook for living. In a culture where the majority of the people base moral decisions on "whatever feels right at the time," it has never been more important than now for Christians to pledge themselves and their children to the standards of the Bible.[1]

It will be impossible to take a stand against the negative influences facing our daughters unless we as mothers are com-mitted to following God and adhering to His commands, reg-ulations, and decrees with all our heart and all our soul, just as Josiah did. When we devote ourselves to the teachings of God's Word, the Bible becomes our parenting manual. Mothers who choose not to parent by God's Word have by default abdicated the raising of their children to the culture at large.

Many of the standard mother-daughter battles are decided in advance when mothers adhere to the standards of God's Word. Christian mothers who choose a position contrary to the standards in God's Word will send a mixed message to their daughters that implies that God's Word is not always relevant in today's world. Children who grow up with compromised standards often believe that rules (even God's rules) were meant to be broken. While it is important that we not get so carried away with following the letter of the law that we lose sight of grace, it is also important that we not take advantage of God's grace to the extent that we ignore the law.

Unlike in the days of King Josiah's reign, the Book of the Law has not been lost. Most likely it sits on bookshelves and nightstands in the majority of homes in America. It is the number one best-selling book of all times. For more than one thousand years it has been the most widely read and circulated book in history. Why then are we experiencing a culture that is all but devoid of its teachings and standards? I believe it is due to the fact that so few of Christ's followers have pledged themselves to follow the teachings of the Good Book. Though Jesus came to establish a new covenant to supersede the old covenant, He also made it clear that He did not come to "abolish the Law or the Prophets" (Matt. 5:17).

What then is the purpose of the law if man is no longer bound by its requirements for salvation? Romans 3:20 states: "Therefore no one will be declared righteous in his sight by observing the law; rather, through the law we become conscious of sin." The Bible is man's moral compass, clearly defining good from evil, right from wrong. Further, it is divinely inspired by God. It contains the one "absolute truth" in this world—Jesus Christ. It will be impossible to counteract the negative influences of our culture unless we use the truths set forth in the Bible as our standard of measure. As mothers, we are called to protect our children from anything that would contradict God's truths and standards. Like Josiah, we must pledge ourselves to the Book of the Covenant and become intimately acquainted with its teachings.

3. Josiah Took Action

After Josiah read the Book of the Law in the hearing of the people and pledged to follow the Lord and keep His commands, regulations, and decrees with all his heart and all his soul, he didn't stop there. The next seventeen verses in 2 Kings 23:4–20 detail steps Josiah took to purge the land of evil influences. He removed from the temple all the articles made for Baal or Asherah and burned them in the fields outside of Jerusalem. He tore down the quarters of the male shrine prostitutes that were in the temple of the Lord and removed the horses from the entrance of the temple that had been dedicated to the sun. He tore down the pagan altars built by his grandfather, Manassah, and smashed them to pieces and threw the rubble into the Kidron Valley. In the town of Samaria, he removed and defiled all the shrines the kings of Israel had built that had provoked the Lord to anger.

After Josiah purged the land of its evil influences, he ordered the people to celebrate the Passover as was written in the Book of the Covenant. In 2 Kings 23:25, Josiah was remembered with this legacy: "Neither before nor after Josiah was there a king like him who turned to the LORD as he did— with all his heart and with all his soul and with all his strength, in accordance with all the Law of Moses."

Before you jump to conclusions and think I am suggesting that you grab a Bic lighter and torch everything in sight that promotes evil, hang in there. Remember, Josiah was king and had the power to remove evil influences from the land. Yet even though we do not have the power of a king, there are things we can do to take a stand against negative influences affecting our daughters. And they are legal! Besides, I don't know what is more frightening: an angry king or an angry mob of mothers who are fed up with half-naked divas, sex-laden television shows, and thong underwear marketed to little girls. Watch out world, here we come.

It's time for the silent majority to speak up. It's time to get off the sidelines and enter the battle. It's time for mothers to give it everything they've got. The powerful influences that reign in our culture have taken advantage of the silence. They have grossly underestimated the power of a united front of angry mothers. Mothers are a sleeping giant, and when the giant awakens, take cover—things are going to change! I believe the giant is slowly stirring and beginning to wipe the sleep from its eyes.

Gone are the days when Christian mothers could assume that good would prevail in the land. The Judeo-Christian value system our nation was founded upon has been replaced with secular humanism run amuck. The current intolerance to Christianity has driven many a faithful mother to her knees in battle. While many battles are won as a result of prayer, the battle against the negative influences in our culture will also require action. When Moses and the Israelite people were fleeing Egypt and were hemmed in at the Red Sea with the Egyptians fast approaching on their heels, Moses told the people to be still and watch the deliverance of the Lord. God's response is found in the verse that follows: "Why are you crying out to me? Tell the Israelites to move on" (Exod. 14:15).

It is not enough to raise our daughters to be prayer warriors. It is not enough to raise our daughters to be lovers of God's Word. In today's world we must also raise our daughters to be activists. First, we will have to become activists ourselves. When we mothers find our voice and speak up, and then further train our daughters to speak up, we will see positive change. As long as we remain silent, the downturn in morality will continue.

Primary Influences Affecting Our Daughters

In order to take a stand against the negative influences facing our daughters, we must first determine where the influences originate. According to George Barna's book *Real Teens*, the two primary influences in the lives of teenagers today are relationships and mass-media experience.

Relationships

According to *Real Teens* by George Barna, teens are more likely to have a meaningful conversation with their friends during a typical day than with either their mother or father. Thus, teens are more likely to consult with friends regarding things of importance to them.[2] When it comes to relationships, mothers can deduce two things from Barna's findings that will assist them in raising their daughters.

1. *Mothers have a great window of opportunity to impart godly standards to their daughters in the younger years when they are willing to listen and have not yet been influenced by the popular opinions of the day.* As girls get older and begin to gravitate more toward their friends, it becomes more and more difficult for mothers to maintain their role as a primary influence in their daughters' lives. When they are little, they think their mothers hung the moon. When they grow into teenagers, they think their mothers are *from* the moon. While it is not impossible to be a primary influence in your daughter's life in her teen years, it will take much prayer and hard work.

2. *If relationships are said to be a key influence in the lives of teenagers, and particularly relationships with their friends, mothers would be wise to train their daughters in the importance of choosing godly friends.* Once a peer group is established, it is very difficult to change a circle of friends. My daughter has been blessed with an outstanding group of friends. She attends a private Christian school, so it was not difficult for her to find godly, like-minded friends. However, my oldest son, Ryan, is attending public school for the first time, and he faced the challenge of choosing a new peer group this past year. His father and I have emphasized the importance of choosing the right kind of friends and have guided him along the way in determining who would make a better "friend" and who would make a better "acquaintance."

Mass Media

When it comes to the influence of mass media, the battle often seems overwhelming. Teens spend an average of four to six hours per day interacting with the mass media in various forms, whether it is music, magazines, television, movies, or the Internet. The typical American is exposed to more than two thousand commercial messages every day at the hands of mass media.[3] Unfortunately, the majority of messages that come at the hands of mass media are almost certain to contradict God's standards set forth in His Word. For mothers, it is an uphill battle to protect their daughters from the onslaught of damaging messages.

We must never let our guard down. We must be fully aware of what our daughters are watching on television, the movies they are seeing, the content of the magazines they are reading, the type of music they are listening to, and how they are using the Internet. While they are under our roof and authority, it is our responsibility to draw reasonable boundaries regarding their access to mass media.

In the remaining chapters, we will cover specific godly qualities that we, as mothers, should be purposeful in passing down to our daughters. In each chapter I will use Josiah's model of examining God's Word for His standards regarding each characteristic and contrast it to the current mind-set of our culture. I will also share tangible ideas of how we mothers can be proactive in opposing negative influences that could compromise the spiritual well-being of our daughters. Don't worry; it's nothing that will leave you in jail stripes picking up trash along the roadside.

If we are going to become proactive in standing against negative influences, let me take this opportunity to emphasize the importance of voting. None of us individually may have the power of King Josiah, but there is power in each vote. It is important to stay apprised of issues up for vote that could compromise the Christian/Judeo standards our country was originally founded upon. The Christian Coalition provides a voter's guide during key election years that highlights the views of candidates running for office and their past voting record concerning many controversial topics that affect the moral fiber of our nation. More information can be obtained at www.cc.org. If we want a moral culture in which to raise our children, we must begin by voting for candidates who stand for morality.

I am also a big fan of www.onemillionmoms.com, and www.onemilliondads.com. Both are Web sites created by the American Family Association that alert mothers and fathers to the sources behind many of the negative influences in the media. With a few clicks of your computer's mouse, you can voice your opinion and cast a vote for morality by sending prewritten e-mails to the media executives responsible for the negative influences. There have been many occasions where companies have buckled to the pressure after receiving a barrage of e-mails from onemillionmoms.com and onemilliondads.com. Remember, there is great power in numbers. These sites provide a great way for the silent majority to speak up and let their voices be heard. The American Family Association has also recently launched a new site for teenagers: www.onemillionyouth.com. If your son or daughter is thirteen years or older, they can practice their activism right now!

As we end this chapter, take the time to go before the Lord as Josiah did and cry out to God concerning the times. Pledge yourself anew to the Book of the Covenant or, rather, the Good Book. Commit to enter the battle and take action. Ask God to prepare you for battle. Psalm 78:9 speaks of the warriors of Ephraim who "though fully armed, turned their backs and fled when the day of battle came" (NLT). Like the men of Ephraim, we too are fully armed; God has equipped us with everything we need for the day of battle. Ladies, the day of battle is here. Fleeing is not an option. In the name of Jesus and for the sake of our daughters, it's time to fight.

Questions for Individual Reflection or Group Study

1. Has there ever been a time when you have wept in the presence of God concerning the times in which we live? If so, what was the stimulus?

2. In your opinion, why is it important for mothers to pledge themselves to the standards of the Bible when it comes to parenting their children?

3. What are some other avenues of information regarding parenting that our culture often pursues?

4. Do you believe it is possible to teach our daughters morality and virtue apart from God's Word? Why or why not?

5. What are your thoughts concerning becoming an activist?

6. If you already consider yourself an activist, give an example of a time when you took a stand against a negative influence.

7. Concerning the influence of relationships, how do you feel about your daughter's peer group?

8. As a mother, what element of mass media concerns you most when it comes to sending messages contrary to God's Word?

9. List some ways God has armed mothers in the battle to oppose the negative influences of our culture.

Part Two

BATTLES WORTH FIGHTING

CHAPTER FOUR

The Dangers of Conformity

*W*hen my daughter was eleven years old, I presented her with a very special ring. I had heard stories about parents giving their preteen or teen daughters rings that represented their daughter's commitment to sexual purity before marriage. While I believe this is a wonderful idea, my daughter was a bit young for such a ring. The ring I gave her was not worthy of a velvet box (I had picked it up at a party supply store for 49 cents). It was a beautiful hue of neon green. When I slipped it on her finger, she winced (with glee?) at the alien face staring back at her. It even glowed in the dark! Lest you think it was meant as a joke, it had a purpose. I presented her the ring as a reminder of a scriptural truth that, if she embraced it, would guide her in making godly choices in the years to come. The ring supports 1 Peter 1:17: "Since you call on a Father who judges each man's work impartially, live your lives as strangers here in reverent fear." The Greek word for the word "strangers" is *paroikia* (par-oy-kee'-ah), which means "foreign or alien resident." I emphasized to my daughter that the world is not our home and that as Christians, we are just passing through en route to our permanent home in heaven. While we are here, we are like "aliens" living in a foreign country. In

John 17:14, Jesus, in His last prayer before He ascended to heaven, tells the Father: "I have given them your word and the world has hated them, for they are not of the world any more than I am of the world."

It will be a natural instinct for our daughters to want to fit in and conform themselves to their surroundings, including their peers. That is not a problem unless their surroundings are opposed to God's standards. As mothers, we must be purposeful in teaching them early on that Christians are called to live in the world without being of the world.

Unfortunately, many Christians have gotten a bit too comfy-cozy in the world, all the while forgetting that their time spent on earth is only a rest stop on the time line of eternity. As our daughters grow older and are faced with situations that could compromise their faith, we must do all we can to equip them in advance to stand firm as alien residents in the world.

When I think of alien residents, I am reminded of Daniel, Shadrach, Meshach, and Abednigo. After Babylon conquered Jerusalem, King Nebuchadnezzar ordered some of the younger Israelite men of royalty and nobility to be brought back to Babylon to be taught the language and literature of the Babylonians. Among these young boys were Daniel, Shadrach, Meshach, and Abednigo. Imagine how these young boys must have felt after being separated from their families and taken to a foreign environment. The boys were to be trained for three years prior to entering into the king's service. The king ordered the boys to consume a daily ration of food and wine from his own table, but Daniel, Shadrach, Meshach, and Abednigo refused the king's food and opted instead for vegetables and water. Because some of the food was forbidden under Jewish law or had been used in sacrifice to false gods and idols, they knew that eating such food would have been against God's will. No doubt, the majority of the young Israelite boys in captivity chose to conform to their new environment, readily accepting the king's rich food and wine. To Daniel and his friends, however, it was a matter of the conscience, something they felt would compromise their faith.

Most likely, Daniel and his three friends were trained early on by their parents to put the Lord their God above all else in the world. Perhaps they had parents who were purposeful in training them to stand for what is true and right, rather than conforming themselves to the culture around them. As mothers, our goal should be to raise daughters who, like Daniel and his friends, refuse to sample the forbidden delicacies on the world's table.

As a parent volunteer at my son's high school, I recently attended a meeting of about three hundred students. The meeting was for a student leadership organization that was given the task of voting for the homecoming theme. I watched with interest as students were given four choices for the theme and then asked to raise their hands when their favorite theme was called. I watched a group of about eight to ten girls as they discussed among themselves which theme they would choose. When it came time for the vote and their preferred selection was called, they raised their hands in unison. As they glanced around the room, it quickly became apparent that their choice was not the popular choice. A few of the girls became visibly uncomfortable and quickly lowered their hands before their vote was counted. I turned to a fellow parent volunteer and said, "Bless their hearts, if they buckle so easily to peer pressure when it comes to the homecoming theme, they don't stand a chance when it comes to drinking, trying drugs, or having sex."

As mothers, we must raise daughters according to Romans 12:2, which says, "Do not conform any longer to the pattern of this world, but be transformed by the renewing of your mind." Unfortunately, this is easier said than done. It is a natural desire for most young people to want to conform to the culture and blend in. This is especially true for our impressionable daughters.

It is our job to help our daughters resist the temptation to conform to the ways of the world by drawing firm boundaries when it comes to possible exposure to ungodly influences. Case in point: In the process of writing this chapter, my thirteen-year-old daughter, Paige, has informed me that I am "the strictest mother in the world." While spending the night with a friend, she called from a video rental store to ask permission to see a PG-13 movie. I looked up the movie in question on an Internet site devoted to screening movies (screenit.com) and discovered that it was labeled "heavy" on sexual content and profanity. When I told her no, she responded with, "Mom, it's not like I'm going to start cussing and doing bad stuff if I see one little movie." I patiently explained that the more a person is exposed to ungodly influences, the more desensitized they become to the same influences in the future. I reminded her that as Christians, we are called to be alien residents in the world and to weigh our decisions according to God's standards. While I realize that I cannot protect my daughter from negative influences forever, my goal is to shield her from the negative influences over which I have control, all the while training her to stand on her own.

I wonder if Daniel or any of his friends ever harassed their moms in their earlier years and told them they were "the strictest moms in the world." Regardless, in the end they would have made any mom proud. Lest you think these boys would only be remembered for their bold stand not to eat the king's food, that was only the beginning. Shadrach, Meshach, and Abednigo faced the biggest challenge of their young lives when King Nebuchadnezzar issued a command for all people to fall down and worship a gold image he had erected. This was not your average gold statue. It was ninety feet high! Their cue to bow down was the sound of the horn, flute, zither, lyre, harp, pipes, and all kinds of music. Further, the king ordered that anyone who refused to fall down and worship the gold image would immediately be thrown into a blazing furnace (see Dan. 3:4–6).

Not surprisingly, Shadrach, Meshach, and Abednigo refused to bow down and worship the image. The king was notified of their disobedience, and they were summoned to come before him. He gave them one more chance to bow down and worship the golden image and reminded them that should they choose not to, they would be cast into the fiery furnace. He further asked them, "Then what god will be able to rescue you from my hand?" (Dan. 3:15).

Now stop for a minute and think about their dilemma. It is human nature to want to conform, yet they overcame that temptation to bow down to the image the first time the song was played. What a picture to imagine the three young boys standing throughout the entire medley of music while everyone else had hit the dirt, most likely at the first blast of the horn. What a shame they were the only three. Would you have remained standing during the first playing of the song? Would your daughter(s) have remained standing? I hope so. If you think you passed the test, hang on a minute. Now put yourself or your daughter(s) in their places the second time around. Ouch. If it's human nature to want to conform, it's all the more so to want to *live*.

I love the boys' response to the king's command when he gave them a second chance to bow down and worship the gold image: "Shadrach, Meshach and Abednego replied to the king, 'O Nebuchadnezzar, we do not need to defend ourselves before you in this matter. If we are thrown into the blazing furnace, the God we serve is able to save us from it, and he will rescue us from your hand, O king. But even if he does not, we want you to know, O king, that we will not serve your gods or worship the image of gold you have set up'" (Dan. 3:16–18).

Now, if that's not radical, I don't know what is. Forget the music and send the orchestra home. No need even to play a chord: these boys had made up their minds. Further, they knew their God was capable of rescuing them, but they did not have the foreknowledge to know whether He actually would. They were prepared to die for God rather than reject Him by bowing down to an idol. How about you? Would you still be standing? Would your daughter(s) still be standing? Most of us, had we made it through the first song still standing, would have complied with the king the second go round after taking one look at the fiery furnace.

King Nebuchadnezzar was so angry with the boys' response that he ordered the fire in the furnace be turned up seven times hotter than normal. In fact, the furnace was so hot that the soldiers, who threw the boys into the furnace, were killed by the flames. Of course, there is a happy ending to the boys' story because they were brought out of the furnace unscathed by the fire. When the king called them out of the fire, he referred to them as "servants of the Most High God" (v. 26). In standing for their God, they publicly gave the one true God the glory and honor He deserved. So too, our daughters should be taught to care more about preserving God's reputation than their own.

I vividly recall a conversation with my oldest son, Ryan, days after the tragic Columbine High School killings in April 1999. A fellow fifth grader at school had told Ryan about one of the students, Cassie Bernall, who when asked by the killers at gunpoint if she believed in God, replied, "Yes."[1] Ryan asked me a very thought-provoking question. "Mom, couldn't she have just lied and said no and then later asked God to forgive her." In answer to his question, I told him that probably a majority of Christians would have said no to the gunman's question had they thought it would have spared their lives. If that question wasn't difficult enough, Ryan's next question will remain forever etched into my mind. He asked, "Mom, what would you want me to do?" Speechless, I was unable to answer his question.

Later that night as I tucked him in, I shared that as I had thought more about his question throughout the day, I had come to a conclusion. I told him that as Christians, our goal should be to come to a point where we love God in such a way that we would be willing to die for Him. I shared with him that in spite of the fact that Cassie was only seventeen years old, many Christians live their entire lives and never come to such a place. With tears in my eyes, I told him that it was my deepest desire that should I ever find myself facing the same question at gunpoint, I would, without hesitation, stand true to my God. I ended by telling him that it is my prayer that my children would also come to the place where they love God more than life itself and stand firm in their convictions.

If our daughters are to stand firm for God in the face of opposition, we must teach them the arduous balance of how to live *in* the world without becoming *of* the world. If we, as mothers, have not come to terms with our own status as "alien residents" in the world, we will have little impact on teaching our daughters this truth. I fear that a great many well-meaning Christian mothers have allowed themselves to be molded and shaped by worldly influences and have sent a message to their daughters that it is possible to be friends with both the world and God. James 4:4 is quite clear when it says, "You adulterous people, don't you know that friendship with the world is hatred toward God? Anyone who chooses to be a friend of the world becomes an enemy of God." Let us not be fooled: God will not play second fiddle in the life of a Christian who has been molded by the world.

How then do we know if we have been conformed to the world and are thus modeling for our daughters a friendship with the world? The second part of Romans 12:2 holds the answer. It says, "Do not conform any longer to the pattern of this world, but be transformed by the renewing of your mind." Renewing our minds involves filtering the world's influences through God's laws and standards. When we become Christians, we must develop a new way of thinking. We are called to surrender control of our lives over to God. It takes a conscious effort to resist the temptation to conform to the world and, instead, conform to God and His plan. God was kind enough to leave us the Bible, His divinely inspired Word, which He intends to be our road map for living. When we develop the habit of filtering our thinking through God's Word, we are able "to test and approve what God's will is—his good, pleasing and perfect will" (Rom. 12:2b).

The truth is, our daughters will be shaped and molded by something. Unfortunately, the majority of them, whether they are Christians or not, will be molded by the worldly influences around them. It is of paramount importance that we, as mothers, abide by Romans 12:2 and, in turn, raise our daughters to abide by Romans 12:2 as well. Without the realization that Christians are called to be "alien residents" in the world, our daughters will, by default, conform to the popular opinion of the day rather than to God's standards.

A recent Barna survey revealed that only 4 percent of teens look to the Bible when making moral decisions in life. A whopping 83 percent said they make moral decisions based on "whatever feels right at the time."[2] In light of this survey, mothers would be wise to realize that a good majority of Christian teens, including possibly our own, will not make moral choices based on principles set forth in God's Word. I used the above survey results for a teachable moment when my son entered public school for the first time this past year. His father and I have emphasized the importance of choosing appropriate friends to be in his peer group. I pointed out that according to the survey, it is not enough to assume that just because someone says they are a Christian or attends church, they will filter their moral decisions through God and His Word when faced with high school temptations. I further pointed out that out of the approximate six hundred students in his freshman class, it is likely that only 4 percent of students—that's twenty-four students—will look to the principles set forth in God's Word when making moral choices. I forewarned him that just as Daniel's friends discovered, standing for truth may mean standing alone.

I am a reality parent, and I want my children to know up front what temptations lay ahead so I can better train and equip them to stand true to their God. To illustrate this point, I warned my son a couple of years ago that there would come a time when he would face the temptation to view pornography. I told him that it was not a matter of *if* he would be tempted to do so, but *when*. I cautioned him that many of his Christian friends would succumb to the temptation because many of them have conformed to the world. I also warned him that if the majority of his peers are making moral choices based on "whatever feels right at the time," be assured that their hormones will cast a sure vote to "go for it." I encouraged him to decide in advance to abide by God's standards and flee sexual immorality (see 1 Cor. 6:18) by refusing to view pornography.

Our daughters must be taught to embrace the truth that there are moral absolutes, i.e., standards of determining right and wrong. The youth of today embrace the lie of moral relativism that says, "What's wrong for you may not be wrong for me, and what's right for you may not be right for me." Under moral relativism, there is no objective standard of right and wrong. Instead, determining right from wrong is a subjective decision that varies from person to person.

Recently, I was on a popular teen Web site and stumbled upon an advice column devoted to answering teens' questions pertaining to sex. The questions were answered by an adult male and female duo that had clearly been indoctrinated into moral relativism and were anxious to propagate its devastating message to teens. One question was from a sixteen-year-old girl who had lost her virginity to a guy she barely knew as a result of her friends teasing her for being a virgin. She claimed that many of her friends had lost their virginity two years ago. She wrote that she now feels ashamed and wishes she could turn back the clock. Here is a portion of the answer she was given: "Next time you have to make a choice like this, make your own choice. You're the only one who knows the right thing to do."[3]

Did you catch that? "You're the only one who knows the right thing to do." They go on to tell her that she should not have been influenced by her friends in making the decision. Let us not forget that regardless of peer pressure, this young lady ultimately made the choice to give up her virginity. In order to make this choice, she must have determined at some point that it felt like the "right" thing to do. Had she instead followed God's moral absolute standard that sex outside of marriage is wrong, she wouldn't be in this pickle. And to think, this is the kind of advice our culture is preaching to our daughters!

Another question submitted to the site was from a sixteen-year-old girl who stated she was six weeks pregnant. Her mother had told her she had three options: abortion, adoption, or keeping the baby. In her question she states that she is against abortion and asks for advice. Here is a portion of the answer given to her on the Web site:

> The only point of view that matters is yours. . . . Even though it's very easy and comfortable to talk to people close to you, in this situation your mom and your boyfriend might be too close to your life to help you make a clear decision. They're not just thinking about what you want; they're thinking about what they want. Someone with a little distance from the situation will help you focus on what *you* want, on what's best for *you*. Which is the only thing you should think about, if you ask me. Good luck, and work quickly. The longer you wait the fewer choices you'll have.[4]

Also included in the answer was a plug to contact the "awesome folks at Planned Parenthood." In spite of the fact that the young woman mentions she is against abortion, the answer makes strong implications that the best choice might be abortion. So much for the previous advice that "you are the only one who knows the right thing to do." If that is true, why didn't they help her eliminate abortion as an option since she stated in her question that she is against it? They even tell her in the text of the answer "the only point of view that matters is yours," yet they disregard her stated point of view that abortion is wrong. Further, they discourage her from consulting with her mom and boyfriend (the father of the unborn child). Unbelievable! She is faced with a life-altering decision that will affect not only her unborn baby but also the lives of her, her mother, and her boyfriend, and these "advisors" recommend that a stranger from Planned Parenthood can better help her determine "what's best for her!" If she decides to keep the baby, I wonder who is more likely to help her raise her child: Planned Parenthood or her mother?!

This poor girl is in this mess because she bought into the principle of moral relativism when she decided to have sex in the first place. What a shame that she did not follow God's moral standards, which are absolute and do not change according to circumstances or the culture.

Popular Christian speaker and author Josh McDowell says in his book *Beyond Beliefs to Convictions* that "our kids need to see our lives as living examples of the wisdom and practicality of a life that is built on biblical principles of right and wrong."[5] He further says, "Most of our kids and many adults, as well, have bought into a cultural mind-set that says we work out our lives independently of God's absolute standards of right and wrong."[6] McDowell points out that this approach does not work in the real world and that living lives based on God's absolute standards is what works.

To possess a belief in absolute moral truths created by God is to possess a biblical worldview. Everyone has adopted a worldview whether they realize it or not. A *worldview* is a perspective on all of life. It is the lens through which we view the world at large, and thus, it determines our value system. The process by which we determine right and wrong is at the very core of our worldview.

Unfortunately, many Christians do not possess a biblical worldview. The Nehemiah Institute has tested teens since 1988 to determine their worldviews. The PEERS test measures understanding in Politics, Economics, Education, Religion, and Social Issues (PEERS). Results from each category are charted on a scale representing four major worldview philosophies: Christian Theism, Moderate Christian, Secular Humanism, or Socialism. From 1988 to 2000, the average scores of students in Christian schools dropped by 30.3 percent and have now crossed over into the range of secular humanism. The average scores of public school students from evangelical families dropped 36.8 percent, ranking them well into secular humanism, not far from socialism. The Nehemiah Institute has determined that based on projections using the decline rate for Christian students, the church will have lost her posterity to hard-core humanism sometime between the years 2014 and 2018. Further, they state that the America we have known for the past two hundred years will be gone.[7]

It is time for a remnant of Christians to emerge who, like Daniel and his friends, have learned the precarious balance of living in the world without becoming of the world.

Unfortunately, just as Daniel and his friends discovered, the right and godly way can also become the lonely way. Daniel's refusal to conform to the world's standards did not hinder him in being promoted through the ranks of Babylonian government. Daniel 6:3 says, "Now Daniel so distinguished himself among the administrators and the satraps by his exceptional qualities that the king planned to set him over the whole kingdom."

Of course, there were some who envied Daniel and set out to find grounds for charges against him. Daniel 6:5 states, "Finally these men said, 'We will never find any basis for charges against this man Daniel unless it has something to do with the law of his God.'" They petitioned the king to issue a decree that anyone who prays to any god or man other than the king over the next thirty days should be thrown into the lion's den. Further, they convinced the king to put the decree in writing, thus making it irrevocable. Read the Scripture that follows to discover whether or not Daniel conformed to the culture that opposed his faith:

> Now when Daniel learned that the decree had been published, he went home to his upstairs room where the windows opened toward Jerusalem. Three times a day he got down on his knees and prayed, giving thanks to his God, just as he had done before. (Dan. 6:10)

I love it! With the windows opened toward his homeland, he prayed and gave thanks "as he had done before." What many do not realize is that some seventy years had passed since chapter 1, when Daniel was abducted from his homeland as a young lad and taken into captivity by the Babylonians. He was now an elderly man faced with a life or death situation. Imagine how easy it would have been to try to justify not bowing down to God for just thirty days! At a minimum, it would have been tempting to at least close the windows and pray out of the public eye! Lion's den or no, Daniel didn't give it a second thought. He simply did what had come naturally for him to do after all these years—go before his God. When word got back to the king that Daniel had defied the decree and had bowed to his God, the king made every effort to save him in spite of his written decree. It was to no avail since the decree was irrevocable. The king was forced to throw Daniel into the lion's den. Still he said to Daniel, "May your God, whom you serve *continually*, rescue you!" (Dan. 6:16). God did, in fact, rescue Daniel by sending an angel to shut the mouths of the lions. Daniel emerged from the pit unharmed, and justice was served when the men who conspired against him were themselves thrown into the lion's den.

If we desire to raise daughters who, like Daniel and his friends, do not conform to the "standards" of our culture, we mothers must also refuse to conform. Like Daniel, we must serve our God "continually." The Hebrew word for "continually" is *tediyra* (ted-ee-ra?), which in its original sense means "enduring," "permanence," or "constantly." Do you live according to God's Word consistently and with permanence, or does your commitment fluctuate such that you, at times, conform to the culture at large? What about your daughter(s)?

If after reading this chapter you have come to the sobering realization that you and/or your daughter(s) have conformed to the "standards" of the culture and have strayed from a biblical worldview, do not be discouraged. It is never too late to get back on track. It will take hard work and effort, but it will be well worth it in the end. If you have gotten off track, talk to your daughter and humbly and honestly confess to her (and God) your sin of conformity to the world, and share your heart's desire to change. If she is in middle school or older and has grown accustomed to loose boundaries regarding the influences of the culture, you can count on resistance. The older she is, the more attached she will be to the world. New boundaries will need to be set to protect her from the influences of the culture, and thus, further temptation to conform to it. Reflect on your high calling as a mother and, if need be, reread chapter 2 of this book to build your confidence and equip you to take a strong stand in the days to come. Remember, you are called to be her mother first and then her friend!

The next five chapters will deal with specific godly attributes that are contingent on the truths set forth in this chapter. Honestly, it will be very difficult to impart the next five godly attributes to your daughter if you and/or she have already conformed to the current culture and the popular opinions of the day. The golden idol of secular humanism has been erected. Many of God's children have chosen the easy way by bowing down to it. I want to raise my children to abide by God's absolute standards consistently and with permanence. Our world is in desperate need of "Daniels." May our children be among the remnant of Christians who will stand for God and His standards, even if it means standing alone.

Questions for Individual Reflection or Group Study

1. Do you view your time on earth as a rest stop on the time line of eternity?
2. Given Shadrach, Meschach, and Abednigo's situation facing the fiery furnace, would you have bowed down to the image? Would your daughter(s) have bowed down?
3. In your opinion, would your daughter fall in the 4 percent of teens who would look to the Bible when faced with moral decisions? If yes, can you think of a specific situation where she has done so? If no, can you think of a specific situation where she failed to do so?
4. Were you surprised by the moral relativism displayed in the answers given on the advice column mentioned on pages 61–63. Were you aware of the prevalence of moral relativism in our culture today?
5. In your opinion, how do you think your daughter(s) would score on the PEERS test when it comes to identifying her worldview? Christian Theism, Moderate Christian, Secular Humanism, or Socialism? How do you think you would score? For more information about ordering the PEERS test, access www.nehemiahinstitute.org.
6. Would you say that you abide by God's standards and serve your God continually, like Daniel? If no, do you desire to? What about your daughter(s)?

CHAPTER FIVE

Passing Down the Formula for True Self-Worth

*P*erhaps the greatest gift a mother can give her daughter is the secret to obtaining true self-worth. Unfortunately, many mothers are unable to give their daughters something that they themselves have yet to discover. As a teenager, I was the type of girl who appeared to have it all. In the pursuit for self-worth, I jumped through every hoop the world held up. I was awarded such titles as cheerleader, class officer, and student council representative. My efforts earned me a coveted spot in the esteemed popular group and a steady boyfriend who drove a flashy Pontiac Firebird with t-tops (remember those?). As I grabbed each of these carrots that the world dangled before me in my endless quest for self-worth, it would satisfy for a time. Yet the boost in my self-worth was short-lived and never enough to satisfy fully. There was a vague awareness in my innermost being that something was missing.

Without an explanation of where true self-worth originates, by default I readily bought into the world's formulas. By the time I got to college, I had a conscious awareness of the futility that comes as a result of basing my self-worth on the world's formulas, but I was not aware of another alternative. My self-paced quest for worth had left me with an eating disorder and had robbed me of my virginity, among other devastating consequences. A major factor in my becoming a Christian at the age of twenty-one was the hope that Christ would address the absence of self-worth and fill the hole in my heart left from the fallout of my quest. I sensed that Jesus was much more than the answer to salvation that leads to eternal life. I sensed that He would provide the key to true self-worth. While my salvation was immediate, I did not experience true self-worth immediately. I grew impatient and frustrated that God's formula for self-worth did not provide overnight results. It was difficult to adjust my way of thinking to God's way of thinking after having been sufficiently brainwashed by the world's formulas since childhood. Like the proverbial dog that returns to its vomit, I ran back to the self-worth formulas that were familiar.

Some ten years later I again came face-to-face with the reality that I had built my worth on sinking sand. The foundation was beginning to crack. My eating disorder once again reared its ugly head, and a general spirit of discontent pervaded my life. Even though I had the knowledge that nothing but Christ could fully satisfy, my actions betrayed my knowledge of this truth. Unfortunately, I was not the lone victim. As a mother, I had unintentionally modeled to my children a willingness to trade God's truth for a lie. Oh, I could preach the truth in regard to where worth originates, but words mean little unless followed by action.

> He feeds on ashes, a deluded heart misleads him;
> he cannot save himself, or say, "Is not this thing in my
> right hand a lie?" (Isa. 44:20).

At the writing of this book, it has been almost a decade since my rediscovery of the formula that leads to true self-worth. Though it has not been easy, with much effort and prayer I have finally come to base my worth on God's one true formula. In addition, I am making up for lost time by actively training my children as to the proper way to define their worth.

What is God's formula for defining one's worth? First, let's take a look at the world's formulas in order to gain a greater appreciation for God's one true formula.

The World's Formulas for Defining Self-Worth

1. Worth = What You Look Like

When sharing my testimony with young girls or college women, I will often make reference to a past struggle in my teen and college years with an eating disorder. After sharing about my struggle, without fail I am approached by young women suffering from eating disorders. I will never forget one such college woman whose appearance alone indicated she was anorexic. She confirmed my suspicion and shared that she had been in the habit of starving herself for many years. She was in need of immediate help, and I encouraged her to contact her mother and discuss options for treatment. To my shock, she shared that she had begged her mother to find her help on several occasions, but her mother had dismissed it, saying she had never looked better. She said that her mother was obsessed with her own weight and had harped on her throughout her childhood for not being as thin as other girls.

While this is an extreme case of a mother encouraging negative behaviors in her daughter, we have probably all been guilty to some degree of unintentionally encouraging the world's formula of "worth = what you look like." Mothers who obsess over their weight, body shape, or appearance in general—and complain in the hearing of their daughters—send a message that supports that formula.

Even if a mother has modeled properly defined worth to her daughter, she will be unable to completely shield her from the world's influence. The formula "worth = what you look like" has saturated our culture and captured the minds of our daughters. As stated in chapter 1, one study of Saturday morning toy commercials found that 50 percent of commercials aimed at girls spoke about physical attractiveness, while none of the commercials aimed at boys referred to appearance.[1] Is it any surprise that the number-one wish for girls aged eleven to seventeen is to be thinner?[2] Our daughters are under tremendous pressure to conform their appearance to the unrealistic ideal created by the culture. Girls who measure themselves against the standard imposed by the culture will quickly become dissatisfied. If our daughters are not raised to understand the true formula for self-worth, they will almost certainly grow up and join the ranks of countless women who forever grumble at their reflection in the mirror.

Mothers who dismiss fashion magazines as harmless entertainment should think twice. Researchers have found that women who looked at advertisements featuring stereotypically thin and beautiful women showed more signs of depression and were more dissatisfied with their bodies after only one to three minutes of viewing the pictures.[3] Our culture esteems beautiful women with perfect bodies. *Sports Illustrated* knows an annual "personality issue" won't sell magazines, but a "swimsuit issue" will. From the time our daughters are young, the world's formula of "worth = what you look like" has permeated their minds through fairy tales with beautiful princesses, fashion dolls with figures that are unrealistic, and magazines touting the latest beauty secrets. Our daughters are left with the clear implication that beauty is the ticket to happiness and fulfillment. If Marilyn Monroe were still alive, she might attest otherwise. The numerous media accounts of beautiful celebrities and supermodels frequenting rehab clinics might also suggest that beauty isn't the answer to true self-worth.

As mothers, we face the daunting task of counteracting the world's formula that "worth = what you look like" lest our daughters become ensnared by the lie. Our first step will be an honest self-evaluation to determine that we have established a balanced perspective when it comes to the pursuit of outward beauty. God certainly never intended that we altogether ignore our appearance. There is nothing wrong with having our nails done, getting our hair highlighted, shopping for the perfect outfit, or exercising to tone up. In fact, we should seek to make the best of what God has given us and, in turn, teach our daughters to do the same. However, when it comes to beauty, are we more focused on shedding the five pounds we gained over the holidays or on having a regular daily quiet time of Bible study and prayer? Are we more focused on getting an extra hour of beauty sleep on Sunday morning or on consistent church attendance? Are we more focused on making our nail appointment or making our weekly Bible study? Most importantly, if we were to ask our daughter if our day-to-day actions indicate that we are more focused on what we look like on the inside rather than what we look like on the outside, what would the answer be?

In *The Virtuous Woman*, I asked readers if they could stand in front of a full-length mirror while wearing their swimsuits and say, "I am fearfully and wonderfully made." Our goal as mothers should be to raise our daughters to say sincerely, "I praise you because I am fearfully and wonderfully made; your works are wonderful, I know that full well" (Ps. 139:14). Of course, they are more likely to respond that way if we can claim the truth for ourselves. It's one thing to acknowledge that you are fearfully and wonderfully made, but do you *know* it "full well"? Mothers who know it full well stand a greater chance of raising daughters who know it full well.

The next step to counteracting the world's formula of "worth = what you look like" is to educate our daughters concerning the reality that bodies come in different shapes and sizes. Some will be tall, others short, some slender, and some heavyset. Some girls were never meant to wear a size 4, and try as they may, their body shape will prevent it. We must remind our daughters that God created each person unique, and to wish they had been born with a different body shape or facial feature is to imply to God that they are dissatisfied with His creation. By failing to inform them of this basic truth, there is a high probability that they will struggle with discontentment if their appearance fails to measure up to the standard of perfection set forth by the culture.

In addition, mothers would be wise to educate their daughters early on to the damaging messages often sent by the media, pointing out how these messages contradict God's standard. Our daughters need to be taught that being "fearfully and wonderfully made" is not conditional upon what the bathroom scale reads, their clothing size, or whether or not they are having a good hair day.

We should remind our daughters of the story of the prophet Samuel, who was called by God to anoint a new king. He thought surely Jesse's handsome son Eliab was the Lord's anointed one. He had "future king" written all over him. Yet in 1 Samuel 16:7, the Lord imparts these words of wisdom regarding outer beauty: "But the LORD said to Samuel, 'Do not consider his appearance or his height, for I have rejected him. The LORD does not look at the things man looks at. Man looks at the outward appearance, but the LORD looks at the heart.'" We must tell our daughters that a beautiful heart will never fade. We should also allow our daughters to hear us praise those who possess true inner beauty. While the world is quick to brand someone beautiful based on physical appearance, Christians should resist the urge and save the label for those who demonstrate beauty that stems from the heart.

2. Worth = What You Do

To this day I can vividly recall the devastation I felt when I was not elected cheerleader in seventh grade. I had readily bought into the world's formula that "worth = what you do," so I had determined that "cheerleader" was a label that guaranteed instant self-worth. For many young ladies, this scenario is all too real. By the time they reach middle school, they have learned what labels will earn the world's applause. Are they talented, athletic, or smart? How many clubs do they belong to? How many times is their picture in the yearbook? When they base worth on what they do, accomplishments and titles become the necessary fix to ensure that they feel like they are something. While accomplishments can *temporarily* quench the desire for worth, the effectiveness wears off with each passing achievement. Surely we all know of people who, in spite of countless achievements, turn up empty in the end.

Unfortunately, most adults have bought into the world's formula that "worth = what you do," so they naturally pass on the dangerous lie to their children. Before I came to depend on God's one true formula for worth, I modeled "worth = what you do" to my daughter. When my daughter, Paige, was two years old, I signed us up for a mom and tot gymnastics class, hoping it would not only serve as an outlet to expend her boundless energy, but also it would give us an opportunity to spend time together. My dreams of mother-daughter bonding were dashed on the first day of class when she pushed me aside and said, "I do it myself." I was banished to the sidelines for the remainder of the class. While other mothers and daughters were somersaulting down the mats, my little one kept wandering over to the three- to four-year-old class to do round-offs and handstands with the big girls. Within weeks, the coaches gave in and put her in the older class, thus beginning her gymnastics career. She loved gymnastics, and it was clear from the beginning that she was a natural at the sport. At the age of five, she was invited to be on a show team that performed at local parades and events. The workouts were rigorous because they were grooming these girls for future competition.

What had started years before as a form of recreation had progressed to three classes and seven hours a week in the gym at the age of five. Paige loved the costumes, performances, and applause, but she was beginning to show signs of stress from the long workouts. She began crying on the way to class and would tell me she wanted to play with her friends after school. Rather than respond to her cues, I found myself giving her pep talks on the way to class about the importance of persistence and hard work. Not a bad lesson to learn, unless of course, you are five years old and want to come home from kindergarten and just be a kid. Finally, after much soul-searching, I came face-to-face with the realization that I was pushing her in gymnastics for all the wrong reasons. I wanted her to excel with the hopes that it would boost her esteem in future years. My own worth had benefited, albeit temporarily, from my success in gymnastics, and I wanted the same for her. I withdrew her from the class and have never regretted it for a minute. Years later, she is casually involved in gymnastics, and her worth is not defined by her success in the sport.

We have all witnessed parents who attempt to live vicariously through their child so they can selfishly say, "That's *my* kid." If you don't believe me, just head on out to the nearest Little League field. Others rationalize, as I had, that pushing their children to succeed provides them with a means to feel worth. This behavior is not just exclusive to the ball field or gym. Many Christian parents put far too much emphasis on their children's grades, believing that good grades lead to good colleges, and good colleges lead to good jobs, and good jobs lead to money and success, and money and success ultimately lead to happiness. While we should encourage our daughters to strive for excellence and work to the best of their God-given abilities, we need to be careful that we do not send a mixed message that emphasizes achievements as a means to define self-worth.

Of what benefit is our son or daughter to God's spiritual harvest if they graduate with honors, attend a great college, and someday nab an elite job but fail to understand their true purpose in life? We do our children a great disservice if we lead them to believe that worth can be found in a prestigious job that comes as a fruit of good grades and higher education. While I desire to provide my children with a good education, my ultimate goal is to raise children who learn to hear the still quiet voice of God and follow His guidance in regard to their future. I often wonder if Christian parents who push good grades as a necessary stepping-stone in landing good jobs would be disappointed if their children were ultimately called into full-time Christian ministry or the mission field.

A survey of teenage girls found that while teenage girls today are more independent and see greater opportunities available to them than their baby-boomer parents did at their age, they have less self-confidence and weaker self-images than their parents' generation.[4] Our daughters are craving a worth that cannot be found through numerous achievements. In order to effectively counteract the world's formula of "worth = what you do," we must first make sure we have not fallen prey to believing the formula ourselves. It will be impossible to pass down the true formula for worth to our children unless we have broken free from the lie ourselves.

3. Worth = What Others Think of You

Perhaps one of the most commonly uttered phrases by a parent to their teen child is, "You shouldn't care so much about what other people think." When girls are young, they look for approval from their parents. They want praise for the picture they drew in preschool or the castle they built with blocks. As they approach late grade school, they begin to look for approval from their friends. It's not just important that they have friends; they must have a *best* friend. To be someone's best friend is a validation that says, "I choose you. You win." Unfortunately, any boost to a young girl's sense of worth is often offset by cruel remarks and backbiting among other girls. As they discover the ups and downs of adolescence, it's not long before they come to the realization that boys don't have cooties. Before long, the desire for a best friend is replaced with a desire for a boyfriend.

Whether consciously or not, our daughters learn what actions will gain approval from others. Unfortunately for many girls, winning the approval of others often comes with a heavy price. For girls who have not learned the true formula for worth, they are easy prey to peer pressures of every sort. As they give in to the desire to please others, it leaves them with a temporary relief that they fit in. The effects, however, are short-term, and "fitting in" to feel worth will leave them feeling worthless in the end. Christian girls are not exempt from seeking worth through the approval of others. Surely we can all think of Christian adults who have yet to shed their people-pleasing tendencies. At times, I still find myself affected by the opinions of others and have to remind myself of the one true formula for worth.

I recall a speaking engagement years ago where I made the mistake of reading the evaluations days after the event ended. Out of more than 150 evaluations, all were praises—except one. To this day I can still remember word for word several harsh comments in that evaluation regarding my speaking style. I've always made it a personal policy to take criticisms before the throne of God and ask Him to show me if there is any truth in the remarks. After doing so, I felt a calm peace that I should disregard the remarks. The evaluation in question contained harsh words not only about me but about every element of the event.

In the end, I came to the logical conclusion that there is usually one sour grape in every bunch. Even so, I would be lying if I told you that it didn't cause me to experience some self-doubt. When I initially read it, I found myself thinking, *Did I miss God in my call to speak? Have I made a mistake?* I seemed not to focus on the more than one hundred praises but on this one negative! Isn't this human nature?

Eleanor Roosevelt once said, "No one can make you feel inferior without your consent."[5] What valuable insight for our daughters—and ourselves. If we are to counteract the world's formula that "worth = what others think of you," we must be active in encouraging our daughters to care less about what others think and more about what God thinks.

God's Formula for Defining Self-Worth

Worth = Who You Are in Jesus Christ

True self-worth can only be found by examining who we are in Jesus Christ. Our daughters need to be taught that while the world focuses on outer beauty and defines worth according to "what you look like," God is more concerned with the heart and what you look like on the inside. When they come to terms with the awesome realization that they were fearlessly and wonderfully made by the Creator of the universe, they will be able to stare at their reflection in the mirror and say, "Beautiful."

Our daughters must also be taught that while the world focuses on achievements and defines worth according to " what you do," God is more concerned with who you are. Try as we may, it is impossible to earn God's acceptance by good deeds. In fact, Isaiah 64:6 tells us that "all our right-eous acts are like filthy rags" to God. The world often puts con-ditions on its approval, but God does not. Our daughters must be warned that if they attempt to define their worth by what they do, it will only offer temporary satisfaction. A day will come when they grow weary of jumping through the world's hoops in order to earn yet another title, label, or accolade.

Finally, our daughters must be taught that if they define their worth according to what others think of them, they set themselves up for heartache. They will never find anyone who spends more time thinking about them during the course of a day than God does. In fact, Psalm 139:17–18 says, "How pre-cious to me are your thoughts, O God! How vast is the sum of them! Were I to count them, they would outnumber the grains of sand." There's not a person alive who can hold a candle to that.

Who would reject the one true formula for defining worth and settle for the world's formulas? Only someone who has failed to understand that God demonstrated His own love for us when He allowed His Son, Jesus, to die for us even though we didn't deserve it. Romans 5:8 says, "While we were still sinners, Christ died for us."

At a recent women's event where I was the keynote speaker, I opened my message with this question: "If you could be anyone in the world, who would it be?" I shared that I had a framed picture of the person that I, personally, would most like to be. I held the framed picture close to myself so the women were unable to see whose picture was in the frame. I asked three volunteers to come up and, one at a time, take a look at my picture to see if, by chance, it was the person that had come to their minds. One at a time, I allowed each woman to take a peek at the picture. One at a time, each one shook her head back and forth, indicating that the picture in the frame was not the person she had chosen. I then held up the framed picture for all to see. It was a framed mirror. How sad that so few women, if given a choice, would choose to be *themselves*. I want to raise a daughter who has discovered the one true formula for worth and, as a result, finds contentment in being herself.

I want to end this chapter with a poem I wrote years ago that recounts my years of misdefined worth and, ultimately, my discovery of the one, true Source of self-worth.

WHAT DO YOU THINK OF ME?

From baby steps and finger paints
and learning how to read,
I proudly asked the world's advice,
"What do you think of me?"

With trophies, grades, and honors
I quickly began to see
the world applauds success and fame—
"What do you think of me?"

"You look great," "You smell good,"
"You've lost some weight, I see."
With high school comes the dating game—
"What do you think of me?"

For boyfriends and promised love,
I traded my purity
and choked back tears and silently asked,
"What do you think of me?"

The world's applause was my reward
when I sought to please,
but the clapping stopped when I missed the mark—
"What do you think of me?"

And now I stand before His throne
burdened by sin and shame.
Beaten and battered by the world,
I call upon His name.

I hold back tears and try to speak
but utter a silent plea.
With downcast eyes, I finally ask,
"What do you think of me?"

I catch my breath as He draws close;
In fear, my knees grow weak.
My heart grows faint as I wait on Him
And then I hear Him speak:

"My child," He said, "the time has come
when you ask the same of Me.
For so long you've sought the world's advice—
What do you think of me?

"Now here we are, My turn has come,
the chance to finally say
exactly what I think of you,
so allow Me, if I may."

Gently, He takes my chin
and raises my face to see.
"My child," He said, "you're beautiful—
you're made in the image of Me!

"The world was quick to judge your deeds,
but failed to tell the rest—
there was nothing you could do
to make Me love you less.

"Before you ever drew a breath,
My name was on your heart,
the Author of your hidden frame
before your life did start.

"You entered this life with pomp and fare
And I held my breath to see,
if those I allowed to care for you
would teach you all about Me.

"An innocent child, your journey began
in this life to find your place.
The world was quick to take your hand
and thus began the race.

"In quiet moments throughout your life
I whispered in your ear,
tender pledges of My love—
I hoped someday you'd hear.

"But the world could offer nothing
to fill your inmost need
and release you from the bondage of sin
and love you eternally.

"My Son was sent to tell the world
of My unfailing love.
A covenant pledged to all mankind
and written in heaven above.

"My Boy was nailed to a rugged cross;
For you, He agreed to die.
Burdened by your sin and shame,
'It is finished,' He finally cried.

"The world could never match My love,
the price was far too high—
for if you were the only one,
My Son would choose to die.

"I've gone to desperate lengths, My child,
to prove My love to you.
I loved you then; I love you now—
Will you love Me too?

"My child," He said, "the choice is yours.
What will your answer be?
It's your turn now—the question is,
What do you think of Me?"

—©VICKI COURTNEY, 1999

Questions for Individual Reflection or Group Study

1. Have you bought into the world's formula: "worth = what you look like"? If so, what consequences did you experience?
2. Is your focus on beauty related more to inner beauty or outer beauty? How about your daughter?
3. In your opinion, are fashion magazines dangerous to young women? Why or why not?
4. Look up Psalm 139:14 and read it aloud. Do you sincerely believe it? Does your daughter?
5. Have you bought into the world's formula: "worth = what you do"? As a parent, do you feel you have modeled this formula to your daughter? If yes, how?
6. Have you bought into the world's formula: "worth = what others think of you"?
7. Would you say that you care more about what others think or about what God thinks? What about your daughter?
8. How do you handle criticism? Does criticism affect your worth?
9. Write below God's one true formula for worth.
10. Would you say that you have come to define your worth according to God's formula? What about your daughter?

CHAPTER SIX

Raising Daughters Who Say "I Don't" Until They Say "I Do"

I remember my first big lesson in the value of patience. Christmas was one week away, and under the tree was a beautifully wrapped present with my name on it. My mom built the anticipation by commenting on it daily. "It's nothing you've ever mentioned wanting, but I hope you like it," she would say. She explained that it was my main present due to the cost. *What in the world could it be?* I wondered. Finally, I couldn't take it any longer. The suspense was killing me. My parents were at work, and I was home alone. I took the gift and carefully unwrapped one end. I slipped the box neatly out of the paper. I opened the box lid and pulled back the tissue paper. Inside the box I found a book (for the purpose of weighting the gift down) and a small velvet jewelry box. I slowly opened the lid to the jewelry box and found a beautiful diamond and gold ring. I put the ring on my finger and it fit perfectly. After sufficiently admiring it on my hand, I put the ring back in its box and carefully rewrapped the present. I placed it in the exact spot under the tree. No wonder my mom was excited about giving me this gift! Instantly I was filled with regret. The gift was meant to be opened on Christmas, but my impatience had gotten the best of me. It wouldn't be the same when I unwrapped it again on Christmas morning. Oh, how I wish I had waited. If only I could go back and do it all over again. . . .

Unfortunately, I failed to learn my lesson with the ring and suffered a much greater loss a year later. I opened another gift early. This gift was from God and was meant for my wedding night. If only I could go back and do it all over again. . . .

One of the greatest challenges our daughters will face is in regard to sexual purity. In a culture obsessed with sex and steeped in sexual imagery, our daughters are inundated with influences that encourage them to cultivate their sensuality. Sensuality sells shampoo, cars, jeans, undergarments, beer, perfume, CDs, movies, and much more. The sexual revolution initiated in the 1960s that trivialized sex as nothing more than an extracurricular activity, has succeeded. The rampant sensuality that pervades our society today is a natural by-product of the downgrading in our society of sex from sacred to secular.

Three decades after it began, the sexual revolution that promised women independence and empowerment has, instead, robbed women and girls of their dignity and self-worth. If there is any doubt as to the damage that has resulted from the sexual revolution of the early 1970s, consider that from 1971 to 1979, the percentage of females aged fifteen to nineteen who had had sexual intercourse increased from 30 percent to 50 percent.[1] From 1978 to 2001, the percentage of high school teens having sex would fluctuate only plus or minus 6 percent.

While the physical consequences of the sexual revolution clearly are devastating, the emotional consequences are even greater. A recent study links depression and suicide to teen sex. The findings are particularly true for young girls, according to the Heritage Foundation, which sponsored the research. The study found that about 25 percent of sexually active girls say they are depressed all, most, or a lot of the time as compared to 8 percent of girls who are not sexually active. The study also found that 14 percent of girls who have had intercourse have attempted suicide as compared to 6 percent of sexually inactive girls.[2]

A separate study called "Hooking Up, Hanging Out, and Hoping for Mr. Right" further proved that our free-sex culture is not without heavy emotional consequences. The study, sponsored by the Independent Women's Forum, found an alarming trend of young people hooking up for casual sex without any promise of commitment or long-term relationships. The report was based on surveys of college women who all but confirmed that traditional dating is a thing of the past. However, the independence and empowerment promised to women by the sexual revolution as a result of no-commitment hookups has left young women feeling anything but empowered. In fact, 61 percent of survey respondents said that a hookup makes them feel "desirable" but also "awkward." Additionally, 83 percent of respondents agreed that "being married is a very important goal for me."[3] The survey results showed that in spite of sexual freedom, most women are incapable of viewing sex as a casual encounter absent of emotional consequences. One Princeton grad summed it up this way: "The whole thing is a very male-dominated scene. Hooking up lets men get physical pleasure without any emotional connection, but for the women it's hard to separate the physical from the emotional. Women want the call the next day."[4]

Another sad statistic resulting from our sexually promiscuous society is the delay of marriage. The average age of men marrying for the first time is twenty-seven, the oldest age in our nation's history. Moreover, the sexual revolution and the trend toward cohabitation offer men many of the benefits they seek from marriage without the obligations and commitment. Between 1960 and 2000, the number of cohabiting unmarried couples in America increased by more than 1000 percent.[5] More than 44 percent of single men ages twenty to twenty-nine agree with the statement that they would only marry someone if she agreed to live together first. Ironically, couples that cohabitated before they were married are twice as likely to divorce as those who did not cohabitate. One reason men cited in the survey for choosing to cohabitate was the convenience of having a regular sex partner. Another reason men cited for living with a woman was that it reduced the risks of sex with strangers. (The familiar saying comes to mind: "Why buy the cow if you can get your milk for free?") In summary, the study concludes, "In the past, of course, men might drag their feet about getting hitched, but there were pressures to wed. Marriage was associated with growing up and taking on male adult roles and responsibilities. Parents expected sons to leave and set up their own household. Now the pressures are mild to nonexistent. Boys can remain boys indefinitely."[6]

The sexual revolution has clearly wreaked havoc on our nation, especially when it comes to women and girls. Our culture has taken the act of sex—created by God for the institution of marriage—and perverted it, equating it to nothing more than a self-gratifying pleasure to be exercised on a whim. The sexual revolution is even considered to be "progress" by many because it supposedly freed women from the "repressive" constraints of the 1950s and before. Let's take an inventory of a few of the results of this alleged "progress" for teen girls today:

1. No more waiting by the phone for that special boy to call. Today girls are in charge. If they want to get a boy's attention, they can pull a Monica Lewinsky and flash him with their thong underwear hanging out the top of their pants.

2. No more poodle skirts and silly sock hops. Today, girls come to the school dances looking like strippers in training. The jitterbug has been replaced with simulated sex on the dance floor.

3. No more old-fashioned dating, where a guy works up the nerve to call a girl and ask her out, meet her parents,

open her car door, pay for the date, and end the date on the doorstep expecting no more than a peck on the cheek. That is so passé. Why would the average guy mess with all that when a good number of girls are willing to "hook up" for a no-strings-attached one-night stand?

So what is a mother to do? For starters, if we desire to raise our daughters to be sexually pure in a sexually impure world, we must be informed. We must have a basic knowledge of what they are being told by their peers, public school, and society in general when it comes to sex. In the next section, I have listed what I believe to be the most common misconceptions among youth today regarding sex. By understanding the common misconceptions and then counteracting them, you will be better able to help your daughter, as well as other teen girls, understand the "why" behind saving sex for marriage.

Even if your daughter has signed a virginity pledge and you are confident that she is committed to sexual purity, I highly encourage you to set aside time to discuss with her the following list of common misconceptions, as well as the accompanying list that addresses the top five reasons girls should save sex for marriage. In doing so, your daughter will be better prepared to counteract the mind-set of the culture and, thus, stay sexually pure. I recommend that you take your daughter on a weekend getaway specifically to discuss sexual purity, using the content of this chapter and any other book you have found helpful. I suggest that you incorporate something fun into the weekend to make it something she looks forward to and reflects back on in a positive manner. Most girls are ready to absorb the following information sometime between their seventh- and eighth-grade year in school or around the ages of twelve to fourteen; however, each girl is different. Most girls will be exposed to information pertaining to sexual activity beginning in middle school. It is best if you can have the "sex talk" weekend with your daughter before she hears lies about sex elsewhere. The only way our daughters can counteract the lies of our culture regarding sex is for us to give them accurate Bible-based information about sex. Mothers should be the primary source of accurate information.

Common Misconceptions Teens Have Regarding Sex

1. Everyone Is Doing It

It would be easy for our girls to assume that everyone is having sex based on the attention it gets in media ads, movies, music, television, and magazines. The truth is that a majority of high school students are *not* doing it. In fact, survey results indicate that sexual activity among high school students is actually declining. In 2001, 45.6 percent of high school students reported that they had had sex. Compare that to 54 percent in 1991.[7] In December 2002, the *Newsweek* cover story read: "The New Virginity: Why more teens are choosing not to have sex." The article says this "wave of young adults represents a new counterculture, one clearly at odds with the mainstream media and their routine use of sex to boost ratings and peddle product."[8] The article further acknowledges that religion plays a critical role, as well as caring parents, a sense of the teen's own unreadiness, and a desire to gain control over their destinies.

Clearly, abstinence-based sex education curricula have had a direct influence on the decline of sexually active teens and have provided many with a common-sense approach to the dangers of sex outside of marriage. In addition, according to a federal survey, 9 percent of boys and 16 percent of girls in middle and high schools say they've taken a virginity pledge.[9]

While this new virginity wave is encouraging, mothers should keep in mind that a majority of high school seniors have had sex by graduation and an overwhelming majority will have sex before marriage. Another caution to mothers is that while virginity pledges have proven to be effective at delaying intercourse, they did not delay it until marriage. According to a study published in 2001 by the *American Journal of Sociology*, virginity pledges were found to delay intercourse only by an average of eighteen months. Additionally, pledges were found to work best among fifteen- to seventeen-year-olds, with little to no effect among older teens.[10]

2. As Long As You Love the Person, It's OK to Have Sex

In a culture where the lines of morality have been blurred, many teens have justified sex as acceptable as long as you *love* the person. Of course, the faulty logic in this rationalization is that teens have the ability to understand properly what "true love" is. Sex did not originate as an act meant to crown "love" except in the institution of marriage. True love says, "I love and respect you enough to wait until we are married." In 1 Corinthians 13:5, love is defined as not being "self-seeking," and abstaining from sex until marriage is seeking the best for the other person. Abstinence provides 100 percent protection against sexually transmitted diseases (STDs); unwanted pregnancies; emotional consequences of premarital sex, including regret, shame, and guilt; and most of all, the spiritual consequence of engaging in an act strictly prohibited by God.

Real love is demonstrated when two people respect each other enough to resist the temptation to have premarital sex based on their concern for the well-being of the other. I cannot imagine a girl out there that doesn't desire to be loved and respected in such a way. In a culture that is focused on self and looking out for number one, it is rare to find displays of the type of love spoken of in 1 Corinthians 13. Abstinence is one such display of "true love."

3. It's Not Sex Unless You Go All the Way

As unpleasant as this topic is to discuss, it is necessary given the times. Oral sex among teens is on the increase, especially among the youngest teens. Surveys indicate that oral sex is viewed by many teens as a less intimate act than intercourse. One Arlington, Virginia, middle schooler explains that it's "a sexual thing that keeps us from having sex."[11] According to Sara Seims, the president of the Alan Guttmacher Institute, kids have convinced themselves that oral sex "is not really sex." An article in *USA Today* reported abstinence programs do not give a comprehensive approach to what teens should "abstain" from and commonly focus solely on abstaining from the act of sexual intercourse.[12]

The article stated that experts cite many factors that have led to the increase among teenagers having oral sex. These factors include early maturation among girls, the media, instant gratification, freedom from pregnancy, the belief it is safe from disease, and the President Clinton/Monica Lewinsky scandal. One fifteen-year-old girl stated in the article, "The consensus in my high school is that oral sex makes girls popular, whereas intercourse would make them outcasts."[13]

In this past year alone, I have had mothers share heartbreaking stories with me concerning this epidemic. One story involved a fourteen-year-old captain of the cheerleading squad who performed oral sex on a boy in a hot tub at a party while her classmates stood by and watched. While speaking at a teen girl's event, another mother shared that the pastor of her large conservative church had received a shocking call from the manager of a local movie theater. The church's youth frequented the theater on the weekends, and the manager had identified them by their T-shirts bearing the name of the church. He expressed frustration to the pastor that his janitors were unable to get the semen stains out of the theater seats and asked the pastor to have a talk with the kids. It was a wake-up call for the parents of the youth. I am alarmed not only at the number of incidences brought to my attention but also the fact that many of the stories involve church kids who should know better.

Physician and radio host Drew Pinsky has a Web site where many teens go to talk about sex. He is hearing from many young teens who engage in oral sex and consider it "just a part of making out." Pinsky also thinks the act is often degrading to young girls. "Their perception is that it is empowering. Really it is the exact opposite. The message they get is this is how to get and keep a man."[14]

4. Condoms Protect Against Unwanted Pregnancies and STDs

This is perhaps one of the greatest travesties is in the misinformation that is commonly taught in sex education regarding "safe sex." Sex is only 100 percent safe when an individual abstains from sex until marriage and marries someone who has also done likewise. Often, the "safe sex" statistics regarding the ability of condoms to protect against unwanted pregnancies and STDs assumes the unrealistic premise that condoms will be used 100 percent of the time with a 0 percent failure rate. Even 100 percent condom use does not eliminate the risk of an STD, including HIV.[15]

Further, teens need to be told that even when condoms are used every time, they can at best only provide a 50 percent reduction in the transmission rates of syphilis, gonorrhea, and chlamydia. Condoms do not appear to provide any protection from HPV (human papilloma virus), which causes 99 percent of all cervical cancer. Clearly, as the Medical Institute for Sexual Health has determined, "safer sex isn't nearly safe enough."[16]

My purpose for presenting these misconceptions among teens regarding sex is to inform mothers so they can equip their daughters with the truths needed to counteract the lies peddled by the culture.

Top Five Reasons Girls Should Wait to Have Sex Until Marriage

In addition to arming our daughters with the list of common misconceptions, we should also provide them with clear-cut

reasons to abstain from sex until they are married. Below are
five reasons girls should wait until marriage to have sex. It
should be emphasized that the first reason alone is reason
enough to abstain. No other reasons are necessary for making
a godly decision. However, some Christian girls, for whatever
reasons, choose to ignore God's truths and principles regarding
right and wrong behavior. They have been taught that sex outside of marriage is wrong, but they have been enticed by the
pleasures of the world. Many godly Christian mothers experience the heartbreaking frustration of a daughter who strays
from God's standards and chooses to have sex outside of marriage. Reasons two through five should provide extra ammuni-
tion for you in your efforts to raise sexually pure daughters.
Even if your daughter would be one to wholeheartedly accept
reason one, I highly encourage you to educate her about the
remaining four reasons as well. She could easily find herself in
a situation with someone who is calloused to God's truth but
who would respond to the other reasons given. The reasons are
short and to the point.

1. Your Body Is Not Your Own; It Belongs to God

First Corinthians 6:18–20 should be memorized by every
preteen and teen before they encounter sexual temptation. It
reads:

> Flee from sexual immorality. All other sins a man
> commits are outside his body, but he who sins sexu-
> ally sins against his own body. Do you not know that
> your body is a temple of the Holy Spirit, who is in
> you, whom you have received from God? You are
> not your own; you were bought at a price. Therefore
> honor God with your body.

Mothers should be purposeful in teaching their daughters
that virginity pledges are made to God and that they cover not
only sexual intercourse but other sexually impure acts as well.
I have spoken with many Christian teens who have justified

that "everything but sexual intercourse is OK." One of the most commonly asked questions I receive from teens is "How far is too far?" I share this answer: "Whatever you would feel uncomfortable doing if Jesus were present—and be assured, He is."

2. A Large Majority of Teen Girls Who Have Sex Regret It

Seventy-two percent of teen girls regret their decision to have sex and wish they had waited.[17] While our culture has brainwashed young women into thinking that "empowerment" includes the right to sex with no strings attached, true empowerment is found in saying no to sex before marriage. Additionally, 89 percent of teen girls surveyed in a 2002 study said their peers (teen girls) feel pressure from boys to have sex.[18]

Mothers need to let their daughters know that it is not uncommon for their daughters' friends to attempt to convince them to have sex if they themselves have had sex. Even though most girls regret the decision, it makes them feel they are not alone in their decision. The saying rings true, "Misery loves company." We need to point out to our daughters that it makes no sense to engage in an activity that brings regret to a majority of girls. Out of the girls who choose to wait until marriage to have sex, 0 percent have regrets. The choice is simple: do they want to be in the category where 72 percent have regrets or 0 percent have regrets?

3. A High Likelihood of a Bad Reputation

Ninety-one percent of teens surveyed said a girl can get a bad reputation if she has sex.[19] The double standard still exists today. Girls may think that boys will like them more if they have sex, but in reality boys respect the girls who choose to save sex for marriage. Some things never change. In the same survey, 92 percent of teens said it is generally considered a good thing for a girl to be a virgin.[20]

One teen boy confirmed the above in a letter to an advice columnist:

> Dear Abby: I'm a guy, 18, and I have something to say to girls who sleep around. They may think they are "hot stuff," but they should hear what is said about them in the locker room. These poor girls think it is flattering to be sought out—that it is a compliment to have sex. Not so! It is cheap and degrading to be used.[21]

4. *One in Four Will Get an STD*

One out of four sexually active teens gets a sexually transmitted disease every year.[22] If your daughter is in high school, have her count up her friends who are sexually active. Ask her to divide that number by four. Tell her that is the number of girls who, according to this survey, will become infected with an STD. Some STDs are incurable, and others can hinder or even prevent young women from bearing children. Remind your daughter that out of any given group of teens who practice abstinence, the number who will become infected by an STD is *zero*.

5. *Forty Percent Will Become Pregnant*

If none of the above reasons is enough to sway a girl from having sex before marriage, perhaps the reality of this one will. A whopping 35 to 40 percent of teen girls will become pregnant at least once by age twenty.[23] Therefore, four of every ten teen girls will be faced with the reality of raising a child, placing a child up for adoption, or having an abortion. Regardless of which choice is made, emotional scars will leave their mark for years to come.

❋ ❋ ❋

When it comes to sexual purity, our daughters will be faced with many challenges. In a society that often appears to be obsessed with sex, maintaining sexual purity can be a rigorous swim upstream. Mothers must educate their daughters that God's call for sexual purity is not exclusive to sexual intercourse but to all sexual activity. Mothers should encourage their daughters to make a personal pledge to God to save sex for marriage, whether they do so through a formal program or privately with God. In addition to the online magazines (www.virtuousreality.com) my ministry launched for middle school, high school girls, and college women, we also have a site (www.virtuepledge.com) where girls can sign a purity pledge online. As well as signing the pledge, the girl can view the countless other girls their age who have signed the pledge. We also send them an annual reminder of their committment and a word of encouragement to keep the pledge fresh in their minds. Mothers will need to remind their daughters on an ongoing basis of the truths listed above through planned times of discussion and unplanned teachable moments.

Perhaps the greatest hope is that teenagers who "feel highly connected to their parents and report that their parents are warm, caring and supportive—are far more likely to delay sexual activity than their peers."[24] Additionally, another study indicated that teenagers in grades eight through eleven who perceive that their mothers disapprove of their engaging in sexual intercourse are more likely than their peers to delay sexual activity.[25] Clearly mothers have great power in influencing their daughters to abstain from sex until marriage. We must clearly articulate to our daughters that sexual activity outside of marriage is wrong and can have devastating physical, emotional, and spiritual consequences. We must also be quick to tell them that God created sex as something beautiful to be enjoyed in the confines of marriage.

We also need to encourage our daughters to seek out friends who share the same commitment to sexual purity. It will help your daughter immensely if she knows she is not alone in her commitment. Further, we should encourage our daughters not to be ashamed of their commitment to sexual purity and to have a willingness to share this commitment with their friends. As more and more teens come forward and share with confidence that they are committed to sexually purity, many others will feel the freedom and gain the strength to do the same.

Questions for Individual Reflection or Group Study

1. How has the sexual revolution influenced the new trend of "hooking up" for sex?
2. If your daughter is old enough, have you had a candid conversation with her regarding sexual activity before marriage?
3. In the list of common misconceptions, which one did you find most shocking? Why?
4. If your daughter is old enough, have you discussed the misconceptions with her? If not, would you consider doing so?
5. In the list of the "top five reasons girls should wait to have sex until marriage," which ones did you find most shocking? Why?
6. If your daughter is old enough, has she pledged to save sex for marriage? If so, was it clear that it included all sexual activity?
7. If your daughter is old enough, have you verbalized to her that sexual activity outside of marriage is wrong? Is she aware of your disapproval?
8. To your knowledge, have your daughter's friends committed themselves to sexual purity?

CHAPTER SEVEN

Dressed to Lure or Dressed to Be Pure

*C*an there be purity without modesty?[1] This question was asked in the September 2001 issue of *Brio* magazine, which is published by Focus on the Family. The answer, of course, is no. Modesty and sexual purity go hand in hand. Given the current prevalence of immodest attire among girls, I felt the subject of modesty merits an entire chapter of this book.

Scantily Clad "Role Models"

The question submitted to the magazine regarding modesty and purity was asked specifically in reference to pop vocalist Jessica Simpson. Simpson is a preacher's daughter who speaks openly about her faith and her commitment to remain a virgin until marriage. She has since married, but her message espousing sexual purity was overshadowed by her immodest, anything-but-wholesome attire.

Prior to her marriage, *CosmoGIRL!* magazine had this to say: "Though everyone knows Jessica's really into being a virgin until marriage, this year she busted out in some decidedly non-virginal outfits." The article goes on to say that one of Jessica's unofficial Web sites even shut down in protest over her new image. Miss Simpson defends her taste for distasteful clothes in the same article, saying, "I think every woman, every girl, wants to feel sexy. If I show a little bit of cleavage, I don't feel guilty."[2] In yet another interview in *Complete Woman* magazine, Simpson says, "My soul and my faith are what's sexy about me."[3]

Miss Simpson's decision to include a rendition of "His Eye Is on the Sparrow" on one of her CDs seems to conflict with her attire and, oftentimes, her behavior. In an interview with *Teen Style* magazine, she was quoted as saying that she likes to "moon" truckers from her tour bus.[4] In response to the backlash she has received from many Christians regarding her skimpy fashion choices, she has this to say on her Web site: "I think the most important thing to remember is who i answer to and that is GOD! At the end of the day, he knows my heart and that is all that really matters! . . . I am still a virgin, i am still a christian, i still am a role model and I take that seriously."[5] Pardon me, Miss Simpson, but I have higher standards when it comes to a role model for my daughter.

Another scantily clad pop sensation who claimed for years that she intended to remain chaste until marriage is Britney Spears. She has since come public with the confession that she is no longer a virgin. Prior to her confession, she was already sending a mixed message to her primary fan base of preteen and teen girls with her skimpy fashion choices. Nora Schoenberg of the *Chicago Tribune* describes Britney as the one "who made the bare midriff safe for the suburban preteen."[6] Britney Spears' biggest fans are girls under the age of twelve.[7] When asked about parents' concern over her being a role model to young girls, she made a distinction between the fantasy world associated with performing, and real life. She also said, "It's up to parents to explain that to their children. I really don't like to be considered a role model."[8] Unfortunately, most young girls are not equipped to separate Britney the pop diva from Britney the person. (In addition, her scanty attire from her "fantasy world" seems to trickle over into her real life more often than not.) Young girls see Britney as famous, rich, and sexy, and they want to be like her. Whether she likes it or not, she is a role model to young girls. Mothers should take note of Britney's clear disregard for the well-being of her primary fan base of young, impressionable girls. If her wardrobe doesn't raise a mother's eyebrow, perhaps the open-mouth kiss she shared with Madonna during the opening performance of the MTV Video Music Awards will. If Britney doesn't want to be considered a role model, the mothers purchasing her products and, thus, supporting her career can certainly arrange to grant her wish.

How sad that Britney and Jessica, among other pop divas, have allowed themselves to be prostituted by the music industry on the altar of the almighty dollar. Like many other women, they have fallen prey to the world's formulas regarding worth. Their wealth and fame will not exempt them from the consequences of falsely based worth. Once their fame dries up (and it will), they will face the sober realization that the industry used them for others' personal gain. While they may be wealthy, their wealth won't be enough to buy back their dignity.

The Fashion Message: Be Sexy

The pop divas, however, are not entirely to blame for the risqué fashion trend. Fashion magazines, movies, and sitcoms have peddled the "be sexy" message to young women for quite some time. Unfortunately, the primary media influencers have now stooped to an all-time low by targeting elementary-aged girls. This negative influence has translated into clothes for little girls that reinforce the message to "be sexy" before most of them even know what the word means. "Being sexy" is equated with female empowerment or "girl power." Our daughters have been bombarded with the "girl power" mantra that associates power and strength with a no-rules attitude in regard to clothes and behavior. The cultural powers-that-be know that "sex sells," and their bottom line is making the sale.

Just recently, I was thumbing through the sale rack in the girl's department of a large department store. Another mother, within earshot, asked the sales clerk for assistance in choosing an outfit for her ten-year-old daughter for an upcoming party. The sales clerk plucked an item off my rack and proceeded to hold up a sheer blouse for the mother's approval. The mother said, "That blouse is see-through." The sales clerk responded, "Have her wear a sports bra underneath. This is what all the girls her age are wearing." By now I am practically hyperventi-lating, as I often do when I feel an onslaught of uninvited words threatening to spew out of my mouth. The floodgates burst, and I belted out: "She's going to a *party*, for heaven's sakes, not a strip club—she's ten years old!" The sales clerk stormed off, and the mother proceeded to thank me for con-firming what she already knew.

Unfortunately, not all mothers agree. Someone has to be buying this stuff or the stores wouldn't be overrun with clothes fit for diva-wannabes. Many mothers have discounted the clothing battle as a battle not worth fighting. Others fear their daughters might not be popular if they don't don the latest skin-baring fashions. I have to prepare myself every morning before pulling into the parking lot to drop off my fifteen-year-old son at the public high school. It's all I can do to refrain from screaming "Cover up, chica!" to some of the girls walking past my car. Where were their parents when they left for school dressed like hoochies? Out of respect for my son, I hold my tongue—for now.

The public high school is not the only place where I've had to hold my tongue. The midriff-baring fashions have even made their way into many of our churches. We need to extend grace to young ladies visiting our churches who may be unaware of appropriate apparel guidelines, but Christian girls and their parents should know better! In an article in the

New York Times called "Dressing Down for Summer Worship," one Catholic church has had to resort to dress-up guidelines for parishioners volunteering as liturgical ministers. The guidelines were developed, the article said, "after a teenage girl walked down the center aisle in a procession at Sunday Mass, holding high the book of the Gospel while wearing short shorts and a midriff-baring halter."[9] At a large Christian youth event where I was a designated parent chaperone, I was appalled to see girls as young as middle school parading around in jeans so tight you could see the date of a dime in their back pockets. Others had bare midriffs or plunging necklines. Clearly, many Christian girls have become desensitized by the saturation of sexually provocative fashions and, thus, have conformed to the world. While I am disappointed to find that many Christian girls have rationalized wearing inappropriate apparel to the Lord's house (or anywhere else for that matter), I find it especially disturbing that most have Christian parents who, for whatever reasons, apparently have turned their heads and allowed their daughters to dress immodestly.

Reasons to Dress Modestly

Lest anyone think my "soapbox" concerning immodest fashions has no foundation, allow me to give three reasons mothers should draw firm boundaries when it comes to the clothes their daughters wear, not just to church, but everywhere. If the clothing battles have started in your home, consider sharing these three reasons with your daughter. They will help her understand why you are drawing a firm line in the sand when it comes to dressing modestly.

1. God

As mentioned in chapter 4, our daughters should be taught early on not to conform to the pattern of this world, but instead to be transformed to God's pattern by renewing their minds. In doing so, they will be able to test and approve what God's good, pleasing, and perfect will is (see Rom. 12:2). In Ephesians 5:8–10, Christians are cautioned to "live as children of light (for the fruit of the light consists in all goodness, righteousness and truth) and find out what pleases the Lord." When finding out what "pleases the Lord" regarding modesty, the best place to look is God's Word, the Bible. It clearly addresses proper apparel for women in public worship in 1 Timothy 2:9–10:

> I also want women to dress modestly, with decency and propriety, not with braided hair or gold or pearls or expensive clothes, but with good deeds, appropriate for women who profess to worship God.

The Greek word for "modest" is *kosmios*. It relates to ornamentation or decoration and it means that which is "well-ordered." One Bible commentary says, "The true idea here is, that her attention to her appearance should be such that she will be offensive to no class of persons; such as to show that her mind is supremely fixed on higher and more important things."[10] The Greek word for "propriety" is *sophrosune*, which means "sanity" or "soundness of mind." Let me translate that for you: "Do the clothes I purchase for my daughter indicate soundness of mind or that I've lost my mind?"

First Timothy 2:9–10 does not go on to specifically outline appropriate apparel, but rather, it cautions against the braiding of hair, gold, pearls, or expensive clothes. Commentaries indicate that women of the East spent much time styling their hair, and according to the prevailing fashion of the time, plaited it with great care, arranging it in various styles and often ornamenting it with silver wires or spangles. The verses are not to be taken literally in the sense of forbidding the wearing of braided hair, jewelry, or nice clothes in today's world. Rather, they stand as a warning not to emulate the women of the world whose attention tends to be devoted to appearance rather than godly deeds. Once again, Christians are called to be set apart from the world.

Women professing to worship God, as the verse indicates, should focus more on adorning themselves with godly deeds.

Barnes' Commentary says this: "It is not appropriate for women who profess to be the followers of the Saviour, to seek to be distinguished for personal, external decorations. If they are Christians, they have seen the vanity of these things, and have fixed the heart on more substantial realities. They are professed followers of Him 'who went about doing good,' and the performance of good works especially becomes them. They profess to have fixed the affections on God their Saviour, and to be living for heaven; and it is not becoming in them to seek such ornaments as would indicate that the heart is supremely attached to worldly things."[11]

When Paul wrote the verses pertaining to the proper apparel of women in worship, his main concern was that nothing would serve to distract from God during a worship service. Everything about a church service should point to God—the music, the sermon, everything. This is not just a caution against immodest clothing but rather, against any outfit that would distract attention from God.

Our daughters (and sons) will have a natural tendency to assume that life is all about them and that their needs and wants come first. As mothers, it is our responsibility to help them make the transition from "it's all about me" to "it's all about God." In choosing to wear clothes that are not pleasing to God, our daughters make a statement that their desire to be "in style" outweighs their desire to show God the awe and reverence He deserves, whether it be in church or anywhere else. When it comes to modesty, mothers should teach their daughters that everything they do, say, and *wear* should bring glory and honor to God.

2. Guys

We all know that when it comes to sexuality, girls and guys are wired differently. Guys are more visually stimulated, while girls are more emotionally stimulated. Case in point: It would make my day to hear my husband say, "Honey, I want to get into your world. Let's go to dinner and talk, and then let's go shopping and get you something." It would make my husband's day (or night) just to see me wear something other than his oversized T-shirts to bed. I think you get my point.

In an Austin, Texas newspaper article addressing immodest fashions, a sampling of boys at a local mall were interviewed and asked what they thought of the girls who walked by wearing the latest skin-baring fashions. One boy suggested that girls "show more to get attention." Another boy perceived it as an "invitation." He said, "They're telling you, 'Come get it.' When girls dress like that, it tells guys they're easy."[12] What mom (or dad), given that news flash, would allow their daughter to leave the house in an outfit that screams "Come and get it!" to every red-blooded male that crosses her path. Sorry, but my daughter is not going to be branded an "invitation" in the name of fashion.

In 1 Timothy 2:9, when Paul exhorts women to dress modestly with "decency and propriety," the Greek word for "decency" is *aidos*, which means "bashfulness (towards men)." In addition, in Romans 14:13–21, Paul exhorts all Christians to avoid actions that would cause others to stumble and fall into sin. Many girls are innocent in their intentions and do not realize that by wearing immodest clothing, they may play a part in causing guys to stumble in the area of lust.

I am certainly not excusing inappropriate behavior among young men. As parents, we should be equally diligent in raising our sons to respect young women and place a higher value on what they see on the inside rather than what they see on the outside. However, we cannot change the fact that guys are visually stimulated and inclined to read more into a racy outfit than a simple expression of fashion.

3. Self-Respect

I vividly recall the first time I had to address the subject of girls wearing immodest clothing with my son Ryan. I was sitting in the stands at his eighth-grade basketball game. The game had not yet begun, and his team was sitting on the bench. The gym was filling up fast as people continued to fill the stands. All of a sudden there was a buzz in the crowd of mothers surrounding me. Their eyes were on an eighth-grade girl who had just entered the gym. In addition to being strikingly beautiful, she was wearing skin-tight ultra-low-rider jeans, three-inch cork wedge sandals, and a shirt small enough to fit my four-pound Yorkshire terrier.

It was clear that she was fully aware of the power of her presence as she sashayed past the team and headed in our direction. She had the walk down as if she had practiced it for hours in front of her mirror. Just to make sure she had accomplished her mission, she glanced back over her shoulder at our boys on the bench and gave them a coy little smile. The mothers in the stands who were aware that I had written a book on virtue turned and looked at me as if I could somehow fix the problem. I looked over at the eighth-grade boys on the bench to see if any of them needed CPR. Their eyes remained fixed on the young lady, and many looked as if they needed to pick their jaw up off the court. Keep in mind: these were boys who went to a Christian school and were accustomed to seeing girls in uniform day in and day out.

Several days later, I broached the subject with my son Ryan. I asked him if he had noticed the girl who had made the grand entrance into the gym. He bashfully nodded that he had (confirming he was an average teenage boy absent of any vision problems). I responded with this: "Bless her heart. She's such a pretty girl. It's a shame she doesn't feel good about herself." My son looked at me with a shocked expression and said, "How do you know she doesn't feel good about herself?" I proceeded to tell him that clothing is like a label on a product. It often gives us information about what is on the inside. I told him that her outfit was sending a clear message that her worth is based on what she looks like, as well as the attention she can get from guys. I summed it up by telling him that my heart breaks for girls who, for whatever reasons, have not come to terms with the beauty they possess on the inside and feel that they have no other alternative but to solicit attention from boys based on what they have to offer on the outside. I further told him that it takes more confidence and inner strength for a girl to buck the current fashion trend and refuse to dress immodestly. When a girl wears modest clothes, it shows that she is comfortable with who she is and doesn't feel the need to "flaunt it" to get attention or "fit in" by wearing the fashions of the day.

My son was left knowing that while most boys would label this young lady "hot," mom had nothing but pity for her. In addition, he probably made a mental note that girls in hoochie clothes are not the kind you bring home to mama. Hopefully, he filed that one away for his dating years.

While many girls, such as the one above, dress immodestly to gain attention from guys, there are some girls who have innocently bought into the current immodest fashion trend without seeing the harm. Many are too young to know that their clothes send a message about who they are on the inside—a message, perhaps, that is not a true reflection of their heart and one they never intended to send. As mothers, we have a responsibility to tell our daughters why modest clothing is important.

What's a Mother to Do?

Now that we're all fighting mad, what can mothers do to counteract the current immodest fashion trend? For starters, we can speak up. You may remember a JCPenney commercial advertising their line of denim hipster jeans. In the commercial, a girl yanks on her jeans and her mother is aghast. "You can't go to school looking like that," the mother says sternly. The mother then pulls the pants down lower. After numerous complaints, JCPenney announced they were pulling the commercial with the following statement: "JCPenney respects the values that parents instill in their children as they develop and, in making this decision, underscored that it considers important the opinions of its customers nationwide."[13] In a similar incident, Abercrombie & Fitch pulled their line of thong underwear for young girls after a barrage of complaints from parents. Never think your voice doesn't matter.

I have scrapped with the clothing industry on several occasions. I recently e-mailed Mervyns department stores regarding a sales flier I received in the mail. It highlighted a brand called "Teaze" for young girls. I have boycotted Abercrombie & Fitch for years and will continue to do so until they quit publishing their controversial catalog that features seminude and nude models hired to look like preteens and teens. Their catalogs include photographic portrayals of fornication, group sex, and masturbation. One past catalog even featured an interview with a pair of female porn stars who freely discussed sexual arousal and sex acts. Tim Wildmon, president of the American Family Association, makes the point that "Abercrombie & Fitch does not merely sell a popular line of clothing—they sell a lifestyle."[14] I, for one, refuse to fund their effort to propagate a casual free-sex message to their target market of youth and college students.

I make it a point to share my disappointment in the lack of modest clothing with store managers, as well as pay my compliments to managers of stores that carry modest clothing. Sometimes I wonder if my little voice will make a difference, but I will persevere for the sake of my daughter—and yours.

Stores are overrun with clothes fit more for future strippers than little girls. A simple mother-daughter shopping expedition can be discouraging. We may have to look harder and shop longer, but it is possible to find clothes for our daughters that are both stylish and modest. Our daughters do not need to look like nuns every time they head outdoors, but they do need to dress in such a way that brings honor and glory to God. I have drawn a firm boundary when it comes to what my daughter is and is not allowed to wear. Paige is allowed to wear most styles of jeans as long as they are not tight and her shirt overlaps her waistline. If the waist in the pants is big, she wears a belt. She cannot wear short shorts or spaghetti strap shirts with exposed bra straps. Clothing conflicts are few because I have carefully supported my modesty standard with the reasons given in this chapter. Dressing with decency and propriety may not earn her a fashion award, but in the end, purity of the heart is the most prized adornment.

Questions for Individual Reflection or Group Study

1. In your opinion, can there be purity without modesty?
2. What are some examples of clothing that you have seen recently that send the message "Be sexy"?
3. Do you personally feel the battle for modesty is a battle worth fighting?
4. Have you witnessed examples of immodest clothing in your church? If so, why do you feel parents allow their daughters to dress inappropriately in church?
5. Is your daughter more focused on adorning herself with the latest fashions or on godly deeds?
6. What is your reaction to the survey of young men regarding girls in immodest clothes and their perception that the girls are inviting guys to "come and get it"?
7. Do you believe the majority of girls who dress immodestly do so to gain attention from the opposite sex or simply to be in style?
8. Have you established a modesty standard for your daughter? If so, what is it?

(If your daughter is older than second grade, consider sharing the three reasons listed in this chapter to support a modesty standard. You may have to revise it to fit her level of understanding and then continue to reinforce the reasons over the years.)

CHAPTER EIGHT

Prince Charming: Fact or Fairy Tale?

*I*t was a lovely wedding. The young bride descended the stairwell of her home with her attendants close behind as they precariously held the train of her dress. The guests down below watched the procession as the handsome groom waited nervously at the bottom of the stairs. Finally, the bride and groom stood together arm in arm. Within a matter of minutes, the pastor presented the wedding vows and concluded with, "I now pronounce you husband and wife." The bride, taking her cue, turned to face her groom, closed her eyes and waited . . . and waited . . . and waited. The groom glanced nervously around the room as if the realization of the kiss had caused him to have momentary doubts. The bride's eyes fluttered open, and through gritted teeth she mumbled angrily under her breath, "You're supposed to *kiss* me." The groom began to fidget, averting his eyes from his beloved bride. Suddenly he saw his way of escape and bolted up the stairs and down the hall to a spare bedroom. The sound of the door slamming echoed down to the foyer, and the crowd erupted in laughter. My four-year-old daughter, Paige, had been jilted at the altar, and better yet, by our pastor's son. She quickly regained her composure and, within minutes, found a replacement groom. A new mock wedding was underway.

Today, years later, we laugh about Paige's earlier days of playing dress-up and, particularly, her preference for playing the part of the blushing bride. It seemed that anytime company came over, any boy within two years of her age was recruited to play the part of the groom, like it or not. Clearly, she had read one too many fairy tales laden with perfect princes and happy endings sealed with a kiss.

She has since outgrown the fairy tales, but she, like other girls, would be hard-pressed to escape the pervasive message that finding your Prince Charming will lead to "happily ever after." The Cinderella story is played out over and over again in romance novels, television, and on the silver screen. Often the top-grossing movies are nothing more than modern-day versions of the Cinderella story. These movies are dubbed "chick flicks" because they are marketed directly to girls and women who have a soft spot for romance. Producers know that grown-up adaptations of the Cinderella story translate into big bucks. Women rationalize that seven dollars is a small price to pay to retreat into fairy-tale la-la land and observe the world as they believe it should be.

Woe to the poor male who is subjected to the latest chick flick. My son recently attended the latest "Cinderella story" with a large group of ninth graders. He came home dazed and confused and offered the following movie review: "All the girls loved it, and I can't figure out why. The entire movie builds up to this couple getting together. By the end of the movie, they finally get together, and all the girls in our group acted so surprised. It was absolutely the dumbest movie I've ever seen." Bless his heart. He has so much to learn.

Each chick flick comes complete with a standard Cinderella, who is perfectly adorable yet noticeably lacking something or, more appropriately, *someone*. Enter Prince Charming (played by the latest Hollywood hunk), who at some point during the movie realizes that Cinderella is, in fact, perfectly adorable and that he alone holds the key to providing her with perfect love and happiness. The remainder of the story centers on his pursuit to capture her heart. Living "happily ever after" is only a kiss away. Mission accomplished. The end. The credits on the screen roll, and in our minds, time stands still with the kiss and the perfect life that we are led to believe will follow.

While there is nothing inherently wrong with our daughters dreaming about the day their Prince Charming will come, we, as mothers, must help them separate fantasy from reality. Buying into the lie that "Prince Charming = happily ever after" can set our daughters up for future disappointment and heartache.

Proverbs 19:22 sheds light on the longing of the heart when it says, "What a man desires is unfailing love." Much of the appeal that keeps women flocking to the fairy-tale themed movies and buying romance novels is the thought that one perfect man exists who will love them unconditionally without fail. Hollywood to Harlequin has figured out how to market to a woman's desire for "unfailing love."

Before our girls feel that first pitter-patter in their hearts that might be misinterpreted as "true love," we must help them define true love. We must educate them to the fact that no man can love them perfectly except One. We must tell them that God purposely placed a desire within their hearts to be loved perfectly and completely. In placing this desire on their hearts, the goal was that they would be drawn to Him as the only source that could satisfy their desire for unfailing love. Unfortunately, many girls and women (including Christians) miss this truth and hold out for Prince Charming.

On a recent morning, I stood in line at my favorite coffee shop. On a chalkboard behind the checkout was written the following question as a brain teaser: "What is the meaning of life?" When it was my turn to order, I politely asked the cashier, who looked to be around college age, "Are you planning to post the answer tomorrow?" She grinned and said, "Well, I suppose the answer is different for everyone." I turned the question back on her and asked her what she considered to be the meaning of life. She quickly said, "The meaning of life is love." I challenged her with the answer, "That's a shame, since the divorce rate is over 50 percent and those who marry usually do so for *love*."

Our daughters need to meditate long and hard on Ephesians 3:17–19 and hide its truth deep within their hearts.

> And I pray that you, being rooted and estab-
> lished in love, may have power, together with all the
> saints, to grasp how wide and long and high and deep
> is the love of Christ, and to know this love that sur-
> passes knowledge—that you may be filled to the
> measure of all the fullness of God.

The deepest desire of our hearts is to be filled to the measure of the fullness of God. Who would not want to know and experience a love that surpasses knowledge? We are well on our way when we acknowledge that only by Christ are we "*filled* to the measure of the *fullness* of God." The words "filled" and "fullness" are derived from the Greek word, *pleroo*, which means to "level up (a hollow)" or "complete." Only the love of Christ can fill and complete the hearts of our daughters (or ourselves, for that matter). Failure to recognize this revolutionary truth leads many girls and women to falsely assume that completion is found in relationships with the opposite sex. Young ladies who falsely assume that relationships can provide the completion their hearts long for are more likely to experience sexual promiscuity, unhealthy dating relationships, and eventually, failed marriages than are those young ladies who understand that only God can fill and complete their hearts through a personal relationship with Jesus Christ.

Young women who recognize that only Jesus Christ has the power to level up the hollow places within their hearts are better equipped to exercise caution when it comes to matters of their hearts. As mothers, we must take advantage of teachable moments to impart and reinforce this critical truth with our daughters. We must be purposeful in defining true love according to God's definition if our daughters are to reject the world's lie that "Prince Charming = happily ever after." Life is not a fairy tale, especially concerning matters of the heart.

Unfortunately, most mothers do not begin to address matters of the heart with their daughters until they are crying on their shoulders after a painful breakup. I was totally caught off guard when my oldest child, Ryan, entered the "going out with girls" phase. I vividly recall chaperoning a seventh-grade dance and glancing out on the dance floor only to see my son slow dancing with a girl and, of all things, enjoying it! I didn't know whether to laugh or to cry. (For the record, I went out to my car, called my husband on my cell phone, and cried!) It was clear that Ryan had more than noticed girls and had entered a new phase of life. I felt grossly unprepared to deal with the hormones that would follow. Part of me was excited to see him start to round the corner of adolescence, and the other part of me wanted to retreat to the days of reading his favorite Dr. Seuss book over and over again.

Now that my daughter has entered the same phase, I don't feel much more qualified, but I have made it my personal mission to remind her often of the love of God that surpasses all knowledge. The challenge seems especially overwhelming when I reflect back on my own tumultuous transition into adolescence. By default, I bought into the fairy-tale lie that eternal happiness was directly linked to finding my Prince Charming or one perfect soul mate. Because I had failed to realize and accept that Jesus Christ was the only one who could level up the hollow places in my heart, I attempted over the years to fill the void in my heart with various worldly solutions, including dating relationships. Many of my Christian friends seemed to be on the same search, somehow failing to grasp how wide and long and high and deep is the love of Christ. Like me, they also longed for filling and completion of their hearts and, instead, settled for the world's counterfeit. Our daughters will run the same risk unless we help them become rooted and established in God's love before they start seeking love through relationships with boys. Our daughters will have a healthier view of relationships with the opposite sex if the process of teaching them about God's love is set in place long before they bat an eyelash at their first crush. In the rest of this chapter, I will cover specific matters of the heart that I discuss often with my daughter.

Crushes, Going Out, and Falling in Love

My daughter's first crush came in seventh grade when I took her and one of her friends to an out-of-state speaking engagement. On the first night, while I was speaking, she and her friend sat on the front row doodling in their journals. After I was finished speaking, I asked her if she had been taking notes during my message, and she giggled bashfully and showed me her artwork. She and her friend had scribbled the name of the drummer from the worship band (a high school boy) over and over in their journals. I chose not to make a big deal about it and later explained that it is natural for many girls her age to have "crushes." Throughout the weeks that followed, I took advantage of teachable moments to impart to her the importance of looking beneath outward appearance and into the heart. She shared that she noticed this boy not only because he was cute but because she could tell that he loved the Lord when he was leading in worship. Not bad for a first crush! Weeks later the crush was long forgotten, and I was thankful I had not gone overboard with my initial reaction.

To Date or Not to Date

When it comes to "going out" or dating, there are many opinions in the Christian community. Depending on the latest best-selling book, attitudes among Christians in regard to dating can change as often as the weather in Texas. Just yesterday teens were "kissing dating good-bye," and today many have decided to "give dating a chance." Based on my own observation of dating trends among Christian teens, I caution mothers to be careful about taking an extreme stand in either direction when it comes to dating. While the antidating/courtship movement has many positive qualities, in reality there are few Christians who, over time, are able to abide by many of the rigid constraints. On the other hand, mothers who allow their daughters to date according to the world's model may subject them to temptations their daughters are not equipped to handle.

I am a big proponent of teens hanging out in groups, especially during the middle school and high school years. This gives them the opportunity to develop relationships with the opposite sex on a friendship level without the trappings of a formal one-on-one dating relationship. However, I realize that a day will come when my children will want to "go out" with one particular person, and depending on their age and maturity, my husband and I will take all things into consideration and seek God's wisdom through prayer in order to make a decision. In the meantime, we will warn our kids in advance of popular dating attitudes that should be avoided. I covered these four types of dating in a Bible study I authored for college women, called *Virtuous Reality*. You will find a slightly revised version below.

Types of Dating to Avoid

1. Dating for fun. Girls should avoid dating someone simply for the sake of saying they are going out with someone.

Dating should not be the forum to explore initial feelings of attraction. Often in high school, relationships begin based on nothing more than an initial physical attraction. As mothers, we should teach our daughters to view dating (when they are old enough) as something they should not enter into lightly. We should encourage them to build friendships and spend time in group settings where they are free to be themselves and get to know people over time.

2. *Dating by emotion.* Most teen girls enter into dating relationships based on feelings more than facts—or God's input. They rationalize that if it "feels right," it must be right. Proverbs 4:23 provides a word of caution that our daughters need to understand: "Above all else, guard your heart, for it is the wellspring of life." Part of guarding their hearts will be learning to trust God more than their emotions. God would not want our daughters to prematurely give their hearts away by swapping casual proclamations of "I love you" in a relationship that years later will most likely be nothing more than a faded memory with "ol' what's-his-name."

Girls who follow their emotions when it comes to dating are more prone to follow their emotions when it comes to sexual temptations. Hormones will often send a message that it "feels right" to pursue natural desires of the flesh. Emotions may also lead them to give in sexually because of the erroneous belief that doing so will strengthen the relationship. Additionally, the culture readily preaches "feelings" as a litmus test for determining readiness to have sex. Mothers need to help their daughters understand the dangers of relying on feelings relative to dating and guide them to make godly decisions based on standards set forth in God's Word and the guidance of the Holy Spirit.

3. *Joined-at-the-hip dating.* Many dating relationships evolve into serious, long-term relationships that, in reality, emulate marriage. Often the couple will give up time previously spent with friends in order to spend more time together.

Girls, especially, are attracted to dating relationships that emulate marriage because of their natural desire for romance and love. This type of joined-at-the-hip relationship almost always leads to physical intimacy due to the amount of time spent together. I am amazed at Christian mothers who facilitate this sort of relationship by allowing their daughters to spend too much time alone with their boyfriends. I realize that there are some high school students who are mature in the faith who have serious Christian dating relationships that remain innocent and sexually pure, but they are the exception, not the rule. I have openly shared with my two older children my regret of having been involved in a serious joined-at-the-hip dating relationship for more than two of my high school years. We spent almost every waking moment together, swapped proclamations of love, and eventually, gave up our virginity for each other. Even though I was not a Christian, I knew in my heart that sex outside of marriage was wrong. Nevertheless, I justified it because I thought we would someday marry and that, somehow, that made it more acceptable. Of course, like so many high school romances, the relationship ended within months of going our separate ways in college, and I haven't seen him since.

4. *"Mission field" dating.* Woe to the young lady who compromises her Christian faith, much less the faith of another, to date a young man who is not a Christian! Second Corinthians 6:14 cautions against Christians being yoked together with unbelievers: "Do not be yoked together with unbelievers. For what do righteousness and wickedness have in common? Or what fellowship can light have with darkness?" If the principle is followed in dating, it could spare our daughters much heartache should the relationship lead to marriage. I am amazed at how many Christian girls (and guys) ignore this verse because it would prohibit them from going out with someone who makes their heart pitter-patter. Many girls innocently enter into dating relationships with non-Christians because they are unaware of

2 Corinthians 6:14. Mothers must be purposeful in sharing the concern about unequally yoked dating relationships *before* their daughters begin dating. Our words of caution often ring hollow once they have fallen for someone who is not a Christian.

Sometimes, however, Christian girls justify dating non-Christian boys as an attempt to be a witness and possibly lead them to faith in Jesus Christ. While it is possible for a Christian girl to lead a non-Christian boyfriend to Christ without her Christian standards being compromised in the process, it is rare that this occurs. I witnessed a youth speaker illustrate this point by asking a student to stand on a chair. The student represented the "Christian" in the dating relationship. He then asked another student to come and stand on the ground next to the chair and for the two to clasp hands. The student on the ground represented the non-Christian in the dating relationship. The youth speaker asked the student on the chair to attempt to pull the other student up onto the chair, while the other student was told to attempt to pull the "Christian" student down onto the ground. It doesn't take a rocket scientist to figure out how this experiment ended. Am I suggesting that we should discourage our daughters from befriending non-Christian boys or providing opportunities for our daughters to invite their non-Christian friends who are boys to church youth activities and camps? Certainly not. However, our daughters will be a more effective light for Christ if they are not entangled in a relationship with the intended target.

When it comes to dating, each mother should go before God in prayer well in advance of the "going out" stage and ask Him for wisdom to develop a plan and standards for dating. Mothers who do not do so have commissioned, by default, their daughters to the world's dating model. When it comes to the biblical charge to "guard their hearts," our daughters cannot be expected to navigate the unstable currents surrounding matters of their hearts alone. Just as we train them in matters of hygiene, nutrition, and other essential life skills, it is equally, and possibly more, important to train them to protect their hearts as the wellspring of life.

As hard as it is to do, mothers must be careful not to send mixed messages in regard to dating by encouraging their daughters to like so-and-so or by implying that "going out" is cute. If we do so, we will play a part in encouraging our daughters to rush into dating before their hearts are ready. We need to follow the admonition found in Song of Solomon 8:4, which reads, "Daughters of Jerusalem, I charge you: Do not arouse or awaken love until it so desires."

Sometimes mothers view attention their daughters receive from the opposite sex as validation of their daughter's worth. We must remind ourselves (and our daughters) that worth is not based on what boys think of them. The only Man who will complete us is Jesus Christ. It is perfectly natural to want to be loved deeply and unconditionally, but mothers should be quick to remind their daughters that no human relationship will quench the desire God placed upon their hearts for His perfect brand of love.

Though it was many years ago, I remember the thrill of being "in love" during my adolescent years. Even today I can hear an old song on my favorite "oldies" station and be quickly transported back to a high school dance and remember exactly who I was dancing with when the song played. Like most every other girl, I longed for the guy who would complete me and make me whole. Several boyfriends later, my heart was broken and still longing for something I had yet to find. The void in my heart was filled when I accepted Jesus and began a relationship with Him. But, even so, it took years for the magnitude of His love to sink into the depths of my heart. Now my heart overflows with gratitude at the mere thought of His sacrificial and unfailing love. Even though I married a wonderful godly man who loves me as deeply and unconditionally as is humanly possible, I know that he can never love me like my Savior does.

My children have been blessed with the privilege of growing up in a Christian home, attending a wonderful Christian school, and regularly attending a Bible-believing church. Sometimes I worry that they hear the message of God's unfailing love so often that they may take it for granted and look to the world's brand of love for satisfaction. I take advantage of teachable moments to point out how Christians can easily make the mistake of substituting the love of Christ with a worldly counterfeit brand of love, only to come up short in the end. While I want them to experience the joy of meeting that one special person, falling in love, and getting married (if God so wills), most importantly, I want them to find their completion in Christ. My prayer is that they come to a place where they are awestruck by His love. Only then will they be able to properly define true love.

Marriage

> For this reason a man will leave his father and
> mother and be united to his wife, and they will
> become one flesh. (Gen. 2:24)

While the futures of our daughters most likely include meeting and marrying their Prince Charming, we must tell them well in advance that he is not responsible for providing them with a life lived "happily ever after." It is unfair and unreasonable to place the large burden for their personal happiness on another person. Beyond the magical kiss comes the sobering reality that Prince Charming belches, channel surfs, and forgets to raise the toilet seat. Living happily ever after is a personal choice. Healthy and happy marriages require time and hard work from both parties. They come as a result of a husband and wife loving each other with the love of Jesus Christ. Our culture and, at times, the Christian community often link marriage as the key to a life lived happily ever after.

While the healthiest of marriages will bring great joy, they will not come close to the satisfaction that comes when we experience the unfailing love of Christ.

Unless our daughters have reconciled that God created the longing in their hearts to be loved and that He provided His Son as the primary means to quench that longing, they are setting themselves up for disappointment and disillusionment in relationships with the opposite sex in the future. It is unreasonable to expect that any mortal man can satisfy a divinely inspired longing of the heart with a manmade brand of love. Let us also be reminded that investing in a healthy marriage will benefit for a lifetime, while investing in a relationship with Christ will benefit for eternity. Jesus made clear in Mark 12:25 that there will be no marriages in heaven. Our daughters must be taught that investing in a close and personal relationship with Jesus Christ is a priority, not to mention a prerequisite to investing in a happy marriage.

The longer our daughters spend basking in the unfailing love of Christ, the better equipped they will be in the future to explore other matters of the heart. As mothers, we have a call to build a fence of protection around our daughters' hearts until the love of Christ has penetrated their hearts through and through. The good news: There is One Perfect Man who will complete them. His name is Jesus. Only when our daughters grasp how wide and long and high and deep is the love of Christ and are filled to the measure of the fullness of God will they discover the meaning of "happily ever after."

End this chapter by praying the following verse for your daughter:

*And I pray that **Paige**, being rooted and established in love, may have power, together with all the saints, to grasp how wide and long and high and deep is the love of Christ, and to know this love that surpasses knowledge—that she may be filled to the measure of all the fullness of God.*

Questions for Individual Reflection or Group Study

1. To what degree, if any, did you fall for the fairy-tale fantasy that a man would make you happy?

2. Have you acknowledged that only Jesus Christ can level up the hollow places in your life and fulfill you?

3. What, if anything, have you used in an attempt to fill the hollow places of your heart in the past?

4. What is your standard for dating? Have you relayed that to your daughter clearly if she is in middle or high school?

5. If your daughter is a seventh grader or older, consider showing her the types of dating to avoid on pages 117–120 and explaining the dangers of each one. If she is in agreement, consider copying them and have her sign a pledge of agreement to keep on hand. Go over them from time to time to remind her and keep them fresh in her mind. Explain that this is part of what it is to "guard her heart."

6. Discuss with your daughter the myth that a man or marriage leads to "happily ever after," and explain the purpose of marriage in the eyes of God. Stress that achieving "happily ever after" in marriage is an individual choice.

7. Write Ephesians 3:17–19 on a note card. Insert your daughter's name in the verse and commit to pray it on a regular basis. Print the verse out for your daughter and help her memorize it. Be sure to explain the meaning behind the verse.

CHAPTER NINE

Sugar and Spice and Not Very Nice

While reminiscing with old friends at my twenty-year high school reunion, a classmate, much to my embarrassment, began to make comments about how mean I had been in junior high school. She recanted in detail things I had said behind her back and times when I had purposely left her out and rallied other girls to do the same. Even though her tone was lighthearted and her words laced with laughter, I found it disturbing that I had earned a spot in the annals of the history of her middle school years as one of the "mean girls." I apologized profusely for my past behavior and chalked it up to the standard adolescent insecurities.

Anyone who doubts that the inclinations of the heart are evil from childhood, as Genesis 8:21 says, need only attend a junior high sleepover where an uneven number of girls are present. Gossip, tears, and backbiting make for full-fledged drama, popcorn included. For many girls, the drama begins before middle school, and many moms are caught off guard as they find themselves ill-equipped to deal with the sudden onslaught of emotions. Let's face it, many of us are still licking the wounds we sustained on the battlefield of adolescent girl politics. While it is an unfortunate, though normal, part of growing up, we mothers need to play an active role in equipping our daughters with biblical principles to help them navigate the minefield.

Girls who are "sugar and spice and everything nice" are made, not born. As important as it is to invest time and effort in training our daughters in vital life skills in their early years, it is equally important to train them in relationship skills that will help lend to their emotional well-being in the adolescent years. And you thought potty training was hard! Add hormones and the standard mother-daughter tensions into the mix (i.e., mom has officially reached "dork" status), and it could be one of your biggest challenges in motherhood. Even if your daughter reminds you on a daily basis of how "uncool" you are, do not dismay. They may roll their eyes in response to your words of wisdom, but chances are, they are listening.

The upside to the adolescent years (yes, there is one) is that it provides our daughters with a practice field for developing basic relationship principles. Even though they will make mistakes along the way, they will find themselves better prepared when it comes to future relationships such as marriage and parenting. Often we invest time into our children's education so that they may someday become a productive member of society. We encourage them to pursue extracurricular activities in order to utilize their talents and teach them teamwork and a sense of accomplishment. However, of what benefit is a degree, a good job, and bookshelves full of awards and trophies if our daughters fail in their relationships with others? With equal devotion we must invest time and effort into training them in basic relationship principles.

Fortunately, we don't have to wing it. Everything we need to raise our daughters to be "sugar and spice and everything nice" and to survive the girls who are "not so nice" can be found in God's Word. Let's take a look at common issues our daughters will most likely face in the precarious adolescent years.

Cliques

If you ask a sampling of mothers with adolescent daughters to say the first word that comes to mind when they hear the phrase "middle school girls," chances are high that a good number will say "cliques." A *clique* is defined as "a narrow circle of persons associated by common interests or for the accomplishment of a common purpose." The definition goes on to state that it is generally used in a negative sense.

One of the biggest needs among adolescents is to "fit in." So strong is this desire that it has led good kids to join gangs or religious cults with wacky beliefs. We should not minimize our daughters' need to fit in, and we should recognize that it is rooted in a desire to be accepted. Girls are, by nature, relational; therefore, they are often drawn to cliques as a means to validate their worth. Our daughters need to be reminded that their true worth is not based on whether or not they are accepted by others; their true identity is in Christ. Girls who accept that their "worth = who they are in Christ" are less likely to be a part of a clique because they do not feel a need to conform to the expectations of others. In addition, we should assist our daughters in choosing friends who share common interests and hold to the same values and beliefs.

I have given my daughter basic information regarding cliques and have warned her of the dangers of associating with such groups. I have told her that a clique is any group that purposely excludes others and acts superior to everyone else. I have also educated her as to the anatomy of a clique. The average clique usually includes one to two strong-willed girls who are the ringleader(s) and a number of other girls who are the "followers." I have warned her that many sweet girls are lured into cliques because they have falsely defined their worth and base their worth on the superficial acceptance of the group. Of course, no clique is complete without one or more targeted victims. Woe to the poor girls who unwillingly become the designated victims.

I think it's important to make a distinction between a "clique" and a group of girlfriends. A peer group does not constitute a clique. We should encourage our daughters to be nice to everyone, but it is unreasonable to expect that every girl will be in the same group of girlfriends. Just as we have natural preferences when it comes to developing friendships, our daughters, too, will prefer the company of some girls over others because of shared similarities. In the grade school years, I made an effort to invite all the girls in my daughter's class to her birthday parties, but as she progressed to middle school, we trimmed down the list to a few close friends. I have told my daughter that there is nothing wrong with preferring the company of certain girls over others, but I also cautioned her to be careful that she and her friends do not allow their peer group to transition into a clique that seeks to exclude others.

What can mothers do to steer their daughters away from damaging friendships? Know who your daughter's friends are and do not hesitate to draw boundaries in her friendships. If you see warning signs that indicate your daughter is in an unhealthy friendship or is part of a clique, take a tough stand and, depending on the severity of the situation, either forbid her from continuing the friendship or limit her time with the friend(s) in question. First Corinthians 15:33 reminds us: "Do not be misled: 'Bad company corrupts good character.'" In the end, protecting her character is more important than allowing her to continue in an unhealthy relationship that could produce devastating fallout in the months or years to come.

Blessed is the man who does not walk in the
counsel of the wicked or stand in the way of sinners.
(Psalm 1:1)

I recall a girl in high school who seemed always to be on the fringe of my peer group. I was in the esteemed "popular group," and at times, it bordered on being a clique. She was a nice and somewhat quiet girl who could have easily found other friends had she been willing to look outside our group. She had somehow rationalized, as many girls do, that acceptance into the popular group would satisfy her longing for worth and value. Even sadder was the fact that it was equally important to her parents that she find her place in the popular group. Week after week she would call girls in the group and invite them to spend the night, often at the prompting of her parents. It seemed that the harder she tried, the meaner we got. How sad that her precious high school years were wasted trying to be friends with girls who did not appreciate or respect her but rather saw her as an annoyance. She deserved so much better, but unfortunately her parents had falsely perceived that "better" was the popular group. Had they seen our résumés, they might have steered her in another direction!

Now, as a Christian, I feel deep remorse over any part I may have played in hurting her. I can't help but wonder if her parents have ever owned the fact that they, too, played a part in hurting her. As mothers, we must encourage our daughters to "walk in the ways of good men and keep to the paths of the righteous" (Prov. 2:20).

Mean Girls

They exist in every city and every state across the country. Every school is overrun with them, whether urban or rural, Christian or public. They are equivalent to the male schoolyard bully, but rather than giving black eyes, they leave bruised hearts. They cause emotional scars so deep that some girls change schools in order to escape the undeserved cruelty. Others find themselves in therapy years later, paying ninety dollars an hour to untangle the web of emotional damage. Mean girls have been present throughout the ages (the Bible is chock full of 'em), but in today's culture they are meaner than ever. The new wave of reality shows has desensitized many to a new breed of blatant in-your-face criticism. This speak-your-mind, tell-it-like-it-is trend has taken the definition of *mean* to the next level. The mean girls of today make the mean girls of my generation look like Pollyanna.

Today, mean girls can spread their venom electronically with the click of a mouse through e-mail, instant messages, and chat rooms. I have been appalled, at times, reading the "profiles" of girls on my son's or daughter's instant messenger buddy list. Many girls, who are "sugar and spice" in person, let their guard down when communicating online and feel comfortable typing things they would never say to someone's face. Some will post comments about other girls they dislike on their online profiles or pass along gossip for all to see. If you don't know how to check your daughter's profile or the profiles of her friends, ask your daughter to show you how. If she is active in sending instant messages, she most likely has a profile she has written about herself. Profiles reveal volumes about the character of a person and can offer mothers great insight about their daughters' friends (and their daughter as well!).

I do occasional spot checks when my kids are online and have explained to them that my purpose is not to check up on them but, rather, to make sure they are not being innocently exposed to offensive material. If I stumble upon online profiles that contain negative comments about others, I don't take the extreme and insist that my child end the friendship. I use it as a teachable moment to talk with my kids about why some kids sometimes feel a need to trash others. If the material is especially offensive (blasphemous statements, porn links, excessive use of expletives, etc.), I encourage my kids to pray and ask God to help them take the right course of action. Sometimes I have been known to send the guilty party an instant message from an anonymous screen name I have created. I kindly ask the party to consider cleaning up their profile and tell them that I am one of their friend's parents. I never disclose my identity, and I am very loving in my approach. In every situation, the child has cleaned up his or her profile immediately and apologized profusely. In some cases, I pass the information along to the child's parents. Youth today are computer savvy and assume that most parents don't have the aptitude to do much more than send e-mail.

Christian girls are not exempt from associating with mean girls or, for that matter, being a mean girl. Even though the tactics of mean girls have changed over time, the typical profile of a mean girl remains the same. Most mean girls base their worth on being in control and exerting power over others, usually by using manipulation or scare tactics. They do not hesitate to ridicule or make fun of others if it promises a laugh. They are constantly on the lookout for supporters who will assist them in their dirty work. Mean girls pick on others in order to deflect negative treatment away from themselves. Deep down inside, mean girls cannot imagine that anyone would ever love or accept them for who they are, so instead, they create a tough exterior that portrays a false sense of self-confidence.

When my daughter, Paige, was in the second grade, we had our first encounter with a mean girl. One evening at bedtime, Paige announced with the passion of a professional drama queen, "I am never ever ever ever going back to gymnastics class again for the rest of my life." I put on my "caring Mommy" face and begged her to tell me what horrible thing had happened to justify the use of so many "never evers" in one sentence. She burst into tears and, through sobs, told me about a girl in her class who "is the meanest girl in the whole entire world times infinite times one thousand." This girl would cut in line in front of her, make fun of her if she didn't do a trick right, and rally other girls to laugh at Paige when she did her tricks. As my little princess shared encounter after encounter, I felt my blood begin to boil, and before she had finished, I had already plotted revenge in my mind. The only question left was, "Do I start with the girl or her mother?" My first instinct was to head downstairs, find the class roster, and give her mom a "friendly" little call. Suddenly, the Holy Spirit took hold of my heart. He reminded me of the passage of Scripture in

Luke 6:27–28, that says to "love your enemies, do good to those who hate you, bless those who curse you, pray for those who mistreat you." *Great,* I thought. *Lord, can't you remind me of that verse* after *I unload on this girl's mother?! How can I possibly "love" a girl who has been so wicked to my daughter? Only superspiritual people can do that "love your enemies" thing, right?*

What happened next must have been a God-thing because I was ready to get my daughter out of bed and give her a crash course in martial arts. Instead, I took a breath and cradled my little girl in my arms while she cried. I told her that as much as I would like to protect her from mean people who say mean things, it would be impossible. I assured her that as long as she was willing to share her hurts with me along the way, I would hurt with her. "It's sad when you hurt, but even sadder if you hurt alone." After spending some time comforting her, I shared with her what the Bible says in regard to "enemies." We started by getting on our knees and praying for that little girl. We asked God to comfort Paige, as well, and to help us know the right thing to do. After we finished praying, I told Paige that we should consider doing something good for this little girl, as Scripture indicates. (Rats! Forget the martial arts!) Paige's face lit up and she said, "I know! Tomorrow I'll make her a card!" The following day, my daughter made this little girl a card with construction paper and stapled a pocket on the inside. She asked me to help her find prizes that we could put in the pocket of the card. We had just celebrated Easter, so we were able to come up with some Easter stickers, erasers, and a pencil.

On the way to gymnastics the next day, we prayed again. The class was two hours long, and Paige had decided to give her the card during the break time. I assured her that I would be sitting outside her classroom, just in case she needed me. Finally, break time came and my daughter glanced nervously at me through the window that separated us. I was beginning to second-guess our Holy Spirit-led response and wonder if maybe it was too late to teach her a few martial arts moves, just in case things got ugly. I watched as she reached into her bag and got out her snack and the card. She walked over to the little girl, who was busy eating her snack. Paige quickly handed her the homemade card and stood nervously beside her as she opened it. My daughter's "enemy" looked at the front of the card decorated with smiley faces, and then she opened it to read the message on the inside. It simply said, "Have a nice day! Love, Paige." Her eyes grew bigger as she spotted the pocket full of treasures inside the card. She quickly turned the card upside down and the loot spilled out before her. I held my breath as I watched the drama unfold. Never would I have predicted what happened next. A smile spread across the girl's face as she jumped up and *hugged* my daughter!

After that, the little girl was no longer mean to my daughter. Weeks later, I was visiting with another mother in the waiting area, and she shared with me that this little girl was from a Jewish family. I stifled a laugh as I thought of the prizes in the card: stickers, erasers, and a pencil—all donning the message "He is risen!" Years later, my daughter and I still laugh about God's double purpose. God used my daughter's hurtful situation to teach us both a lesson about forgiveness and loving our enemies, while at the same time, planting seeds in a little girl's heart about the Source of forgiveness.

> If you love those who love you, what credit is that to you? Even "sinners" love those who love them. And if you do good to those who are good to you, what credit is that to you? Even "sinners" do that. (Luke 6:32–33)

Gossip

Years ago, a friend of mine was deeply wounded when she discovered that her best friend had betrayed her trust and shared confidential information related to problems she had experienced in her marriage. Proverbs 16:28 accurately predicted the outcome: "a gossip separates close friends." The fallout was devastating and brought an end to a longtime friendship. Both women are Christians, yet the sad story proves that in spite of numerous warnings in Scripture regarding gossip, many women will fail to heed the warnings and succumb to the temptation to trade choice verbal morsels.

Gossip has often been treated in the church as a "little" sin, but in Romans 1:29–31, it is listed among such serious sins as unrighteousness, fornication, wickedness, covetousness, maliciousness, envy, murder, deceit, backbiting, hating God, despitefulness, pride, boasting, and inventing evil. Ouch. Clearly, God views gossip as a serious matter. Unfortunately, our culture not only condones gossip but often encourages it. Many of the teen girl's fashion magazines feature columns on celebrity gossip and treat gossip as a standard aspect of life for girls. In a culture that embraces moral relativity, where each person determines what is right and wrong, gossip for most people is barely a blip on the radar screen of "wrong" behaviors. Because of this, our daughters can expect some ribbing from friends if they take a stand against gossip on the ground that it is "wrong." As mothers, we need to remind them that they are set apart from the world and that gossip is a sin. Scripture warns of the dangers of the untamed tongue.

Some of the following verses are good to go over with your daughter. I have gently encouraged my daughter to consider posting some of the verses by our computer as a reminder when she is sending instant messages back and forth with her friends. Chatting with friends online can easily become a breeding ground for swapping the latest gossip. In fact, my daughter has been sent instant messages that contain comments that were shared in confidence by another girl to the sender. It is common practice for girls to cut and paste comments and send them on to others. I have told my daughter that this is no different from the old-fashioned version of swapping gossip by secret telling or passing notes and have encouraged her to take a stand when someone sends gossip her way.

Interestingly, the word used for "gossip" in the King James Version is "whisperer." When I think of "whisperer," I think of the game of gossip, where you pass a phrase around a circle of people by whispering it. Of course, when the last person states what she heard, it is usually not remotely close to the original phrase. The end result of real-life gossip is no different. Our daughters should be on guard for phrases that start with "Did you hear . . ." or "I probably shouldn't say this . . ." If they offer a gentle response that heads off gossip, it won't take long for other girls to figure out that they are not a willing party when it comes to gossip. I have told my daughter that if she finds herself on the receiving end of gossip on a regular basis, then the ones passing it along clearly see her as a willing party.

Following, are Bible verses that deal directly with gossip, or misuse of the tongue:

- Proverbs 10:19: When words are many, sin is not absent, but he who holds his tongue is wise.
- Proverbs 11:13: A gossip betrays a confidence, but a trustworthy man keeps a secret.
- Proverbs 12:18: Reckless words pierce like a sword, but the tongue of the wise brings healing.
- Proverbs 18:8: The words of a gossip are like choice morsels; they go down to a man's inmost parts.
- Proverbs 18:21: The tongue has the power of life and death, and those who love it will eat its fruit.
- Proverbs 20:19: A gossip betrays a confidence; so avoid a man who talks too much.
- James 3:9: With the tongue we praise our Lord and Father, and with it we curse men, who have been made in God's likeness.

I am particularly convicted by the fact that no matter how diligent I am in training my daughter to resist participating in gossip, if I model otherwise to her when it comes to my own life, my words will ring hollow. James 1:26 says, "If anyone considers himself religious and yet does not keep a tight rein on his

tongue, he deceives himself and his religion is worthless."
I would be devastated if my failure to practice what I preach
caused my daughter to question whether or not "my religion is
worthless." No doubt, it is a verse to hold this mom accountable! Yet, to err is human, and I often blow it. There have been
many times when I have experienced conviction from God
over words I have spoken, and the Holy Spirit has prompted
me to make it right by contacting the person to whom I passed
along forbidden morsels and ask forgiveness. This is a painful
exercise, but it makes me think twice the next time I am
tempted to gossip. If my daughter witnesses me partaking in
gossip, it is my responsibility to own my sin, tell her I was
wrong, and ask her forgiveness.

Jealousy

Beware of the big green monster called "jealousy." If your
daughter has reached the middle school years, you have most
likely encountered this monster in abundance. By high school,
it has usually morphed into the Loch Ness monster. As our
daughters struggle to find their identity, they often measure
themselves against others. In doing so, it becomes easy for girls
to pick out qualities and things they see in others that they wish
they had themselves. We mothers can certainly relate to the
temptation to want someone else's dress size, another's income,
another's house, car, personality, obedient children, romantic
husband, and so on and so on. Our daughters are no different.

We can help our daughters avoid the bite of the big green
monster by reminding them that they are unique creations of
God and that He has equipped them with unique talents and
abilities to be used for His good and glory. As they come to
believe in the person God created them to be, the longing
to be like someone else will dissipate. Unfortunately, many
adult women fail to reach this point. For the mothers who have
not, it will be impossible to pass this truth along to their
daughters. Jealousy is one of many manifestations of a girl's

(or woman's) mistakenly defined worth. A true mark of properly defined worth is the ability to take joy in the attributes and achievements of others. Rare is the woman who is comfortable enough with who she is so that she can sincerely rejoice with another woman who accomplishes or attains something that she had wanted for herself.

As I mentioned in an earlier chapter, I remember vividly a personal encounter I had with jealousy in the seventh grade. It was the beginning of the school year, and cheerleading elections were being held. Nearly one hundred girls signed up to try out in front of a panel of judges. The judges would pick fifteen girls who would then try out in front of the student body to determine who would fill the six coveted spots. My life goal at that point was to be a cheerleader. My best friend and I had been practicing cheers and holding mock tryouts since fifth grade. Her older sister was a cheerleader, and when I saw her in her uniform, I knew it was my destiny. If you're from Texas, you understand—cheerleading *rules!*

Everyone thought I would make it because I had two things going for me: back handsprings and popularity. I was confident that my skills would get me past the judges and my popularity would earn me the student vote. Unfortunately, the script did not play out according to plan. I will never forget sitting on the gym floor among the multitude of seventh-grade girls as the cheerleading sponsor read the names of the fifteen girls who had made it past the judges. I waited and waited to hear my name, but when the last name was called, my name was not among the fifteen. My best friend had made it past the judges, but I had not. I was devastated. Never had I imagined the story would turn out that way. I was overcome with jealousy, and when it came time for the student body vote, I could hardly stand to see my best friend up on stage realizing my dream. Rather than rejoice with her, I was focused on myself and consumed with envy. When it came time to circle six names on the ballot, I did not circle her name.

All the same, she made the squad and I feigned the obligatory excitement. In the months that followed, it cut to the core to see her in the uniform and cheering at the games. We used to walk home from school together, but now she had to stay after school for practice. I would walk home alone, sulking over my status as a noncheerleader. The next year we both made the squad, and her genuine excitement for me made it all the worse when I reflected back on my shameful actions the year before.

As mothers, we should help our daughters process moments of disappointment before they transition into jealousy. As they come to realize that God does not play favorites and has a unique plan and purpose for each person, it will free them up to rejoice with others. More importantly, as they witness mothers who are content with themselves, content with their circumstances, and sincerely content when others prosper, they will take notice.

When it comes to raising girls who are "sugar and spice and everything nice," there is no secret formula. We can do our part by equipping them with biblical truths, setting boundaries, and encouraging them to take the high road in difficult situations. In the end, it will be up to our daughters to determine whether they choose nice or not so nice. As a past middle school not-so-nice girl, my prayer for my daughter is that she will be remembered at her twenty-year high school reunion as one of the "nice girls" who reflected the love of Christ to others.

Questions for Individual Reflection or Group Study

1. Were you more of a "mean girl" or a "nice girl" during your middle and high school years?
2. Do you agree that girls who are "sugar and spice and everything nice" are made, not born? In your opinion,

what part can mothers play in encouraging their daughters to be nice?

3. Has your daughter had a negative encounter with cliques? If so, have you taken the time to discuss the dangers of associating with a clique?

4. Have you and your daughter ever exercised the privilege of praying for an "enemy" or "mean girl"? If so, what was the situation? What was the outcome?

5. Which of the verses on page 135 concerning gossip and the tongue did you find particularly convicting? Is gossip a problem for you? If so, what are you doing to remedy the problem?

6. Does your daughter struggle with jealousy, or is she able to rejoice with others when things go well for them?

7. Have you been vulnerable with your daughter concerning difficulties in your adolescent years and encounters you experienced at the hands of "girl politics"?

Part Three

ARMING OUR DAUGHTERS FOR BATTLE

CHAPTER TEN

A Heritage in God's Word

Your statutes are my heritage forever;
they are the joy of my heart.

—PSALM 119:111

*I*n the December 1948 *Ladies' Home Journal*, the following ad for Oxford Bibles can be found: "This Christmas . . . give your child the Bible. A fine Bible is the rightful inheritance of every young American. As the Pilgrims drew from it their dream that this nation might be founded in freedom . . . and Roosevelt his dream of the Four Freedoms for all the nations of the world . . . so from its pages today's young leaders will build tomorrow."[1]

Coincidentally, I received my "rightful inheritance" for Christmas as a gift from my grandparents when I was ten years old. I remember holding the children's Bible tenderly in my hands that Christmas morning, somehow sensing I had been given a prized possession. Even though I wasn't raised in the church, my mother had been faithful in telling me many of the familiar Bible stories, so I knew this was no ordinary book. As I carefully turned the crisp pages of my new Bible, I came upon a picture of Jesus in a green meadow that was covered with spring flowers. Surrounding Him were children of all sizes and colors. He was holding one boy's hand and had His arm around a young girl who was in the process of presenting Him with freshly picked wildflowers. The picture presented Jesus as an approachable and caring friend to the children. The children's faces danced with laughter, and their eyes sparkled with adoration for their new friend. I recall looking at that picture and longing to know this Jesus.

I set out with determination to read my new Bible from cover to cover in hopes of finding out more about Jesus. Unfortunately, my interest dwindled by Genesis, chapter 5, when I encountered the endless series of "begats." In my middle school and high school years, I remember retrieving the Bible off my bookshelf from time to time when I was experiencing a time of difficulty, confusion, or sadness. I would sit on my daybed, brush the dust off the cover, and open the Book, somehow knowing it contained the remedy for my distress yet not quite sure where to look. My Bible had a very basic concordance in the back that listed helpful verses to look up in times of need. I remember being particularly comforted by Psalm 23 and memorizing it. How odd that I was comforted by the Shepherd's leading in my life, though I had yet to formally meet Him!

Far from the path of God and heading to college, I packed that Children's Bible in my suitcase, sensing I might need it over the course of the next four years. As I moved from place to place during my college years, it always found a home tucked away in my top drawer. One evening during my junior year, I was overwhelmed with sadness over a breakup with a boyfriend and a life that, overall, seemed empty and directionless. My roommates were out and the apartment was strangely silent. I opened the drawer and found the Bible tucked away in a corner. I fluffed up the pillows on my bed and sat down, holding the Bible in my hands. Just touching it seemed to calm my anxious heart with a strange and settling peace. I opened it up randomly and began to read. I cannot recall what I read that night, but whatever it was, it brought me an instant dose of comfort. I read for quite some time until tears began to roll down my cheeks. Unable to read the blurry words any longer, I closed the Bible and cried out to God for help. It was on that evening that I felt a clear presence of God in the room. Somehow I knew that everything was going to be OK and that my life was going to take a drastic turn. For years God had tried to get my attention, and for years I had snubbed Him. That night, for the first time, I acknowledged that I needed Him.

I didn't have a clue how to take the next step, but it didn't matter because God took over from there. He wasn't about to let me out of His grip after years of drawing me to His path. Days later an old boyfriend called out of the blue to tell me about a decision he had made to rededicate his life to Jesus Christ. He explained that he had been a committed Christian in his years prior to college but had fallen away over the last several years. Duh, he was dating *me* during those years! He went on to share how he had grown weary of the partying life and had returned to the ways of his Christian faith. He invited me to go to church, but I declined. My grandparents also became more persistent in inviting me to their church, but I declined. Even though I had finally acknowledged that I needed God and knew church would be a positive step in the right direction, I wasn't quite ready to leave my old ways of life.

A couple of months later, my old ways were in full swing as I headed to South Padre Island for spring break. My "God moment" had dissipated, and once again I found myself filling the void with alcohol and parties. Little did I know, God was not far. One evening, while drinking on the beach with friends, I could hear faint singing off in the distance. The songs were familiar choruses I remembered singing in my years of Young

Life in high school. I participated in Young Life not for spiritual reasons but for the simple fact that that's where all the cute boys were. The songs had tugged at my heart from time to time, but not enough to woo me from the wayward path I had chosen at the time. However, on this night it was different. I felt uneasy hearing the choruses. I laughed along with my friends at the absurdity of a Christian college group that would choose to spend their week at South Padre Island, a primary spring break party destination. Yet a part of me felt drawn to them. Still I resisted the call of God on my life and tempered my confusion with more alcohol.

The next morning I was standing in the parking lot with a group of friends. We were busy loading a cooler with more beer in preparation for another day on the beach. Out of the corner of my eye, I noticed a guy approaching our group but gave it little thought. As he neared our group, he seemed to make eye contact with me. He passed by my friends and walked directly up to me, as if he were some sort of messenger on a mission. He was holding something in his hand and held it out to me and said, "Would you like to know about God's love?" More concerned with maintaining my image than hearing a sermon, I quickly responded, "No, but would you like a beer?" and pointed to the cooler. I will never forget the look of dejection on his face as he walked away with his head bowed and echoes of laughter ringing in his ears. He probably mumbled a prayer for my lost soul and questioned his decision to spend his spring break vacation attempting to bring the good news to people like me. Little did he know, seeds were planted that morning as a result of his faithful obedience.

Several months later, after much persistence, I finally accepted the invitation from my old boyfriend to go to church. Coincidentally, it was the same church my grandparents attended. While there, an upcoming retreat for college students was announced, and my old boyfriend talked me into signing up. One of the items on the packing list was a Bible, so when it came time to go, I faithfully pulled my children's Bible out of the drawer and packed it away in my suitcase.

At that retreat I stopped running from God and gave my heart and life to Jesus Christ. Finally, I came face-to-face with the great Shepherd of the Twenty-third Psalm I had memorized so many years before. Like the children in the picture of my first Bible, I longed to know this Jesus. After the event, my grandparents, who had given me the children's Bible some ten years earlier, replaced it with a grown-up study Bible after they heard the news that I had given my life to Christ. I embarked on a new life with my new instruction manual in tow. My old children's Bible sits on a shelf in my office as a reminder of how my legacy in God's Word began.

If our daughters are to build a legacy of faith, God's Word must be their blueprint. I can recall my daughter, Paige, toddling into Sunday school at the age of two, carrying her hardcover Bible storybook. As she has gotten older, it has since been replaced with a study Bible geared to teens. In order to experience the power in God's Word, she must develop a habit of tapping into this "power source" on a daily basis. Bibles that are opened, read, studied, memorized, weathered, and worn produce the best results. Ephesians 6:17 reminds us to take up "the sword of the Spirit, which is the word of God." God has equipped our daughters with this "sword" to battle the culture. As mothers, it will be our responsibility to teach them to arm themselves for battle with the Word of God.

The more I speak to Christian youth and college students, the more convinced I become of the need for mothers to teach and train their daughters in the importance of the Bible and its intended purpose. While the Bible is the best-selling book of all times, it is often thought of as merely a book, rather than the inspired Word of God. In a culture that preaches moral relativism and political correctness, it is easy even for Christians to lose sight of the fact that absolute standards of right and wrong behavior are contained in God's Word. If we are to equip our daughters to stand against the moral relativism they will face, we must help them become convinced that the Bible is not a book, but the accurate revelation of God and His standards to mankind. It is best if we can do so before seeds of doubt are planted in their minds by the culture.

All Scripture is God-breathed and is useful for teaching, rebuking, correcting and training in right-eousness, so that the man of God may be thoroughly equipped for every good work. (2 Tim. 3:16–17)

The Bible Is God's Revelation of Himself to People

In our culture today, the Bible is rarely acknowledged; and when it is, it is often referred to as a man-made compilation of stories and spiritual insights or opinions. As mothers, we must be active in teaching our daughters that the Bible is no ordinary book. The Bible contains God's words, truths, standards, and principles. It reveals His character and presents His message of love and redemption to all mankind. Second Timothy 3:16 clearly states that all Scripture is God-breathed. God inspired more than forty authors to write the Bible over a span of fifteen hundred years. It was written in three languages, in thirteen countries, covering three continents. The Bible is broken into two testaments, the Old and the New.

The Old Testament contains the recorded fall of man away from God because of man's sin, man's resulting need of for-giveness (redemption) from God, and a system of presenting sacrifices offered to God to meet His qualifications for re-demption. Before the coming of Jesus Christ, God's message was revealed to the Jewish people through prophets, chosen by God to be His mouthpiece.

The New Testament documents the birth, life, death, and resurrection of Jesus Christ, the Messiah (Redeemer) about whom the Old Testament prophesied. It is a continuation and, ultimately, fulfillment of the redemption story introduced in the Old Testament. The Bible documents God's offer to mankind of His forgiveness of sins through Jesus' sacrificial death on the cross. In doing so, God extended grace (unmerited favor) to all people. Every person is given the free will to accept or reject this divine offer. In the New Testament, God's message of redemption to people is relayed through Jesus Christ rather than through chosen prophets.

> In the past God spoke to our forefathers through
> the prophets at many times and in various ways, but
> in these last days he has spoken to us by his Son,
> whom he appointed heir of all things, and through
> whom he made the universe. (Heb. 1:1–2)

When Christ died on the cross as a payment for the sins of all who had lived and would ever live, a new covenant between God and the people was established. With this new covenant, it was no longer necessary for people to present an animal sacrifice to God as a means for receiving temporary forgiveness for their sins. Under this new covenant, Jesus became the ultimate and final sacrifice. Of course, the most beautiful part of this redemption story is that God sent His Son, Jesus—who was fully man and fully God and perfect in every way (see Heb. 4:15)—to die for all mankind. No greater display of love exists. I make it a habit to tell my children that the Bible is God's love letter to each and every person. It reveals His heart to the people and unveils His eternal plan for all mankind.

In Frank Harbor's book *Reasons for Believing*, he makes the excellent point that the Bible could not be the invention of men because "such a theory of human conspiracy is ruled out by the vast time span involved in the writing of the Bible. Not only would such a conspiracy require someone who could make up the fictitious story, it would require legions of actors and civilizations to act out the story in history. No human conspiracy could supervise such a one thousand-year project."[2]

If our daughters fail to see the Bible as divinely inspired by God, it will become nothing more to them than just another good book containing simple suggestions brought by mere people. However, if they come to realize that God is, in fact, the Author of the Bible, they will much more easily understand and accept that the Bible is the final authority in all matters of life. The Bible trumps the popular opinions of the day brought by our culture. It changes everything.

The Bible Is Reliable

Can the Bible be trusted as the accurate source of God's truth? You bet! Christians do not need to check their brains at the door when it comes to supporting the validity of the Bible. While the unity of the Bible is one factor that supports the validity of the Bible, there are other supporting factors as well.

Archaeology

There is an overwhelming amount of archaeological evidence to support the validity of the Bible. For example, a recent study of ancient Jericho concluded that the walls did tumble down as the Bible indicates. More than twenty-five thousand archeological sites have been discovered that connect to the Old Testament period. These discoveries have provided much evidence to support hundreds of scriptural assertions. In fact, not a single archaeological discovery has contradicted or disproved a biblical assertion.

Prior to the nineteenth century, there were many facts in historical accounts of the Bible that could not be confirmed. As a result, severe attacks concerning the legitimacy of the Bible were launched in the nineteenth century. It was claimed that people and places recorded in early Scripture were legend, not historical fact.

Shortly after these attacks began, an explosion of archaeological finds took place. Was this mere coincidence? I don't think so. The existence of places and people described in the Old Testament were proved credible with the discoveries of ancient civilizations in Egypt, Babylonia, Palestine, and Assyria.

The Bible continues to be historically verified by archaeology. It is exciting to think of the archaeological finds that will occur in the years to come that will further support the validity of God's Word.

Consistency of Scripture over the Years

When I participate in friendly debates concerning Christianity, one of the most common arguments I hear against the Bible is that it could not possibly reflect the original documents since it has been translated so many times over the years. I love debating people on this point because it simply isn't true. I find that most people who use this argument have absolutely no evidence to support their statements and are only repeating what they have heard others say over the years. Like most people, I do not possess extensive knowledge pertaining to scriptural consistency, but what little I have has always proved to be more than enough to silence the critics I encounter. Before my children leave for college, it is my goal to provide them with some basic facts regarding the consistency of Scripture in order to equip them with a ready defense.

New Testament defense: The great scholar F. J. A. Hort concluded from a lifetime of studying early documentary evidence that "not more than one-thousandth part of the New Testament is affected by differences of reading." He added that there were only insignificant variations in grammar or spelling between various documents.[3] More than 24,000 partial or complete copies of the New Testament exist today. When compared to other documents of ancient writings, it is nothing short of amazing. Homer's *Illiad* has 643 existing ancient copies of the original, while both Aristotle's and Caesar's works have 9 to 10 ancient copies of the original. No one doubts their validity and they are extolled in public schools and universities.

Equally amazing is the short span of years between the original writing of the New Testament and the creation of the first copies. The first copy appeared only twenty-five years after the original. Compare this to Homer's *Illiad*, for which there is a time span of five hundred years between when it was written and the first copy of it. Most other famous ancient books have longer spans, and none comes close to the New Testament's twenty-five-year time frame. No book in antiquity can hold a candle to the New Testament when it comes to the number of existing manuscripts or the number of years between the original writings and copies.

Old Testament defense: The year 1947 marked one of the greatest archaeological finds of all time with the discovery of the famed Dead Sea Scrolls. The scrolls were contained in ancient jars found in caves in the valley of the Dead Sea. They date back to between 150 BC and AD 70. In this significant find, the entire Book of Isaiah was found, as well as fragments of every book of the Old Testament except Esther. When the scrolls were compared to the Masoretic text written some one thousand years later by Jewish scribes (from which our Old Testament of today is derived), it resulted in remarkable accuracy. This is not surprising given the fact that great care was taken by scribes in copying the original text. Because they believed they were documenting the Word of God, they were devoted to accuracy. They were known to wipe the pen clean before writing the name of God, copy one letter at a time, and count the letters of the original and the one copied to confirm accurate transmission. In some cases, if an error was found, the entire copy was destroyed.

Fulfilled Prophecy

Dr. Hugh Ross, a well-known astrophysicist, says that out of approximately twenty-five hundred predictions contained in the Bible concerning the future, some two thousand have already been fulfilled. Every one of these has been fulfilled in detail without a single error. Dr. Ross has calculated that the probability of two thousand predictions coming true without error are 1 in 10^{2000} power.[4] Science considers any probability greater than 1 in 10^{50} power as impossible. So how was it possible? There is only one explanation: God, who knows the future, inspired the writers of these predictions to write them down in text that today constitutes the Bible.

One well-known prophecy contained in the Old Testament concerns the destruction of the city of Tyre. Hundreds of years earlier the prophet Ezekiel claimed the city would be destroyed and the ruins scraped off and dumped into the sea, never to be rebuilt. It happened exactly as predicted.

Some of the most amazing examples of fulfilled Bible prophecy are those concerning the birth, death, and resurrection of Jesus Christ. For example, Isaiah 52–53 and Psalm 22 contain details about death by crucifixion some hundreds of years before this form of execution was ever practiced.

Why is it important to teach our daughters about the validity of the Bible?

When it comes to support for the reliability of the Bible, please know that entire books have been written that document evidence supporting the validity of the Bible. It is impossible to do the subject justice in one chapter, but hopefully, this will provide you with enough basic information to aid you in teaching your daughter about the validity of the Bible. I have seen troubling statistics that indicate that a majority of Christian youth who go to college will stray from their faith. There are many factors that cause Christians to stray in college, but one that I hear over and over again in my ministry to college students is that they are caught off guard when their Christian beliefs are challenged, especially, the belief that the Bible is the inspired Word of God. As a result, they are ill-prepared to defend their beliefs, and many begin to have doubts as to whether their beliefs are true.

It is not enough to teach our children to believe in Jesus because the "Bible says so." We must go a step further and teach them *why* we are confident the Bible was written by God through men. "The Bible says so" won't cut it as an effective argument in defending Christianity, matters of morality, or wooing someone to the Christian faith. It may have worked fifty years ago when most people accepted the Bible's divine origins without question. Today, the Bible is thought by many to be nothing more than a compilation of man-made opinions. It's not a matter of *if* our daughters will be challenged in regard to their beliefs concerning the origin of the Bible but *when*. If our daughters begin to doubt the reliability of the Bible, they will likely also begin to doubt the validity of the claims of Jesus, standards of right and wrong, and characteristics of God that are recorded in the Bible. Such doubt will weaken the very foundation of their Christian faith.

The Bible Is Relevant
The grass withers and the flowers fall, but the word of the Lord stands forever. (1 Pet. 1:24b–25a)

Most books have a short lifespan. Most books that topped the charts ten years ago are long forgotten today. The Bible, however, is still remembered today, even though it was written thousands of years ago. To top it all off, it is the best-selling book of all time. When you stop and think about the longevity of the Bible, it is nothing short of a miracle. God's principles set forth in His Word are timeless for all ages. Our daughters need to know that God has left us the Bible as an instruction manual for living. God's standards, principles, and truths will act as a compass to steer them in the right direction (even when Mom is not there to help!) and give them the ability to filter right from wrong, good from evil, and wisdom from folly. Of course, in order for our daughters to partake of this wonderful treasure, they will need to recognize its value and come to depend on it as a source of sustenance in their daily lives. How do we raise daughters who crave time in God's Word as much as they do food and water? We make the Bible a central part of their lives from the time they are young.

If your daughter is young (two to five years old), get her a good picture Bible and read her the timeless Bible stories in it. Let her carry her Bible to church and develop a sense of ownership. Look for teachable moments to remind her of how the stories and principles in God's Word still apply to life today. I remember my mother taking the time to explain the meaning behind a rainbow in the sky. Since that time, I have always known that it is a symbol of God's promise to His people. When sharing Bible stories or Scripture, be careful to emphasize the positive, rather than use it as a tool to manipulate good behavior. Children should never be told, "God is angry with you" or "God is watching you, and He's not happy." It is critical in the early years that children develop a healthy, positive image of God as a loving heavenly Father who watches over and takes care of them.

If your daughter is older (six to twelve years old), it is a good idea to help her develop a model for having a quiet time. My husband or I read our daughter an age-appropriate Bible devotion book at bedtime that focuses on a Bible passage, applies Scripture to life situations, and ends with a few thought-provoking questions. We are fairly consistent, but on nights when homework is heavy or extracurricular activities run late, we just say prayers. If you do a devotion with your daughter at night, be careful that it doesn't run too long, or she may become overwhelmed. Also, make sure it is age appropriate and deals with issues that are common to your daughter's age. This will help her connect the dots when it comes to taking Scripture and applying it to her everyday life. Also, as she gets older, encourage her to highlight meaningful verses in her Bible or write them in a journal.

If your daughter has reached the teen years (thirteen to eighteen years old), she should be independent enough to self-initiate a quiet time. This is a difficult age because you want to encourage independence in your daughter, but in doing so, she may not be as consistent in her quiet times as you would like for her to be. I don't berate my daughter if she slacks off in her Bible reading, but I do gently remind her if I notice that some time has gone by without her reading the Bible. It is no different from training her in other life skills. I still have to occasionally remind her to take a jacket to school, brush her teeth, feed the pets, do her homework, etc.; therefore, it is not out of the ordinary for me to occasionally ask, "Have you read your Bible lately?" If she says no, I don't shame her or put her on a guilt trip. I have explained to her that she is the one to suffer when she does not prioritize spending time in God's Word. Her relationship with God is no different from a relationship with a close friend. In both cases, the relationship will cease to be close if she ceases to spend time with her "friend."

Great is the investment in teaching our daughters that the Bible is the revelation of God, reliable, and relevant. In doing so, we equip them with a basic understanding of the origin and purpose of God's Word. If you were to ask the average mother what hopes she has for her children, the majority would say they desire their children to be happy. Believe it or not, according to a study by Barna Research Group found in the *Austin American Statesman*, reading God's Word on a consistent basis can actually lead to a more positive outlook on life.[5] Specifically, the study revealed the following:

1. Eighty-two percent of regular Bible readers described themselves as "at peace," versus 58 percent of those who said they never read the Bible.
2. Seventy-eight percent of regular Bible readers said they felt "happy" all or most of the time, versus 67 percent of nonreaders.
3. Sixty-eight percent of regular Bible readers said they were "full of joy," versus 44 percent who said they never read the Bible.
4. Eighty-one percent of regular Bible readers said they were satisfied with life in general, versus 63 percent of those who don't read the Bible.

5.   Ninety-four percent of regular Bible readers believe that life has a clear purpose and meaning, versus 76 percent of nonreaders.

What's Your Favorite Book?

The most important factor when it comes to raising daughters who love God's Word will be modeling that we, ourselves, love God's Word. I was touched by an account in Beth Moore's book *Feathers from my Nest.* This section was actually written by her daughter, Melissa, as she reflected back on a difficult time in her high school years. She had bought into the lies of the culture concerning beauty and image. She was up for homecoming queen and had put her energies into the perfect dress, a perfect tan, and a perfect body (albeit, by starving herself). She said:

I was everything that Hollywood was telling me I had to be. I was deathly skinny, popular, and completely miserable. The morning after the event was over, I woke up to the smell of warm blueberry muffins. I walked downstairs only to see the norm. My mom was sitting in the dining room doing her "quiet time." Her quiet time was the time she spent alone each day. Without catching her attention, I watched her. She was in her old, faded pink robe. Her hair was a mess and she did not have on a hint of makeup, but she looked so beautiful. I had watched her do her "quiet time" for seventeen years, but it had never caught my attention like this. There was something about that day that was absolutely brilliant. Her face was radiant. I saw her sitting there in her chair and knew that she was truly satisfied. I wanted what she had.[6]

Does your daughter witness a mother who is truly satisfied because of the time you spend in God's Word? Does she know the source of your satisfaction? She may not state that she "wants what you have," but rest assured, she is watching.

When my youngest son, Hayden, was in first grade, he surprised me with a homemade gift for Mother's Day. It was a booklet that had pages stapled together. Each page contained a different picture he had drawn of me, along with vital (and sometimes incriminating!) information. As I flipped through the pages, I praised his artwork, even though it confirmed that the Courtney family does not possess an artist trait in the gene pool. In every picture, I was wearing a giant muumuu-looking tent dress and my hands were five times bigger than any other part of my body. In the latter pictures, I was missing fingers, as if he had grown weary of all the attention to detail. One page asked, "What is your mom's favorite thing to do with you?" Hayden had written, "Play baseball with me," and true to form, I was still wearing the muumuu, with a bat in hand.

The last page asked the question, "What is your mother's favorite book?" I was relieved and partly amused that Hayden had answered, "The Bible and her own." At the time, I had just finished writing *The Virtuous Woman* Bible study, so my time invested in writing the book had not gone unnoticed. Fortunately, he had also noticed me reading my all-time favorite Book, the Bible. Warmth and laughter filled my heart when I saw the picture on the page. Grasped in my oversized six fingers, I was holding a book labeled "The Bible."

Questions for Individual Reflection or Group Study

1. Do you model a love of God's Word to your daughter?
2. Does your daughter have a basic understanding that the Bible is God's revelation of Himself to the people?
3. Have you ever discussed the reliability of the Bible with your daughter?

4. Have you discussed the relevancy of the Bible with your daughter?

5. What do you currently do to model a quiet time for your daughter?

6. What steps (if any) might you take to help your daughter develop a habit of spending time in God's Word?

7. What teachable moments have you taken advantage of to help your daughter better understand God's Word?

8. If asked, what do you think your daughter would say is your favorite book?

CHAPTER ELEVEN

A Heritage of Prayer

Prayer is the alternating dance between "faith that moves mountains" and "thy will be done."

—C. S. LEWIS

*W*hen I was a little girl, I remember reciting a prayer rhyme with my mother at bedtime: "Now I lay me down to sleep; I pray the Lord my soul to keep; if I should die before I wake, I pray the Lord my soul to take." I remember lying in bed pondering the meaning of the words. It wasn't exactly the kind of prayer that left you enveloped in a calm peace. The end of the prayer was a bit unnerving and led me to wonder if death was a common side effect of bedtime. In spite of my initial confusion over the meaning of the words, thus began my communication with Almighty God.

As I got older, I began to question the purpose and benefit of prayer. Was God even there? Was He listening? Before long, my prayers became infrequent, reserved only for times of true emergency. Emergencies that merited 911 flair prayer included a date to the homecoming dance, that annoying zit that might not go away before picture day, cheerleading tryouts, tests for which I was unprepared, and an occasional plea that my annoying younger brother (or mother) would vaporize into thin air. My prayer life was a one-way dialogue where I submitted my wish-du-jour to the magic Genie in the sky, somehow imagining He had nothing better to do than entertain my list of shallow self-centered requests. If I failed to receive the answer I had hoped for, it further cemented my belief that if God was on the receiving end of my requests, He was not listening to me.

I had presumptuously assumed that God would match His will to my desires. He was the vending machine and I was the customer. The machine would occasionally malfunction and fail to deliver the goods. Playing the part of the frustrated customer, I began to wonder if it was worth it to put another coin in the slot. Regardless, I continued my sporadic correspondence with God through prayer. Deep within the depths of my soul, I wanted to believe that there was a loving God on the receiving end of my petitions.

When I accepted Christ as my personal Savior at the age of twenty-one, I began a two-way relationship with God and sealed it with a prayer. In my newfound desire to know the God of my salvation, prayer became a natural by-product of my new relationship. My previous shallow and self-focused prayer life became more God-directed than me-directed. Prayer was my lifeline to my Maker.

Prayer, simply put, is conversing with God. The more our daughters converse with God, the more in touch they will be with His intended purpose for their lives. A consistent prayer life can act as a safeguard against mediocrity and a tendency toward a lukewarm Christian faith. Well-balanced "conversations" with God include both talking to God and listening to Him. After all, how good would a relationship with a friend be if our conversations always boiled down to a long to-do list for the other person.

When I taught fifth- and sixth-grade Sunday school, we would end our time with praises and prayer requests. The students often struggled to think of praises, and when they did, most were for good grades on tests, sports victories, upcoming school holidays, and other things of direct benefit to them. Their list of prayer requests was always much longer, and for the most part, equally as self-focused as their praises.

The ACTS Model

Philippians 4:6 says, "By prayer and petition, with thanksgiving, present your requests to God." There is certainly nothing wrong with asking God to do things for us, but there are other aspects of prayer that are also important. One of the simplest and best prayer models I have found that leads to a well-balanced prayer life is the ACTS model. ACTS is an acronym that stands for Adoration (or praise), Confession, Thanks, and Supplication (making requests of God for others or ourselves). I have adopted the ACTS model of prayer for myself, and my husband and I have diligently taught the ACTS model to our children and have utilized it as part of their bedtime ritual. We began teaching them this model of prayer when our youngest child was four years old. By the time he was six, he could tell you what each letter stood for and give a basic definition of each word. We found the ACTS model to be very user-friendly for our young children.

At bedtime, my husband or I would start prayer time with our children by speaking words of adoration (praise) to God the Father. We then allowed our child to do the same. We would go back and forth, taking turns on each aspect of ACTS. This way, it helped our kids understand what each aspect of ACTS means and helped them put it into practice. Once they began to grasp praying the ACTS model, we would have them pray it themselves. When parents pray with their children, they assist them in having a heart-to-heart talk with the Father by placing their hand in the hand of the Almighty. The goal is that as our children get older, they will take the initiative to reach for His hand on a regular basis. If you do not have a well-balanced model of prayer either for yourself or your daughter, consider implementing the ACTS model.

Adoration

It seems only fitting that prayer to the Holy God should begin with acknowledgement of His divine characteristics and attributes. Our relationship with God is put into the proper perspective when we, the creation, submit in awe and reverence to our Creator. It is an expression of faith when we take the focus off our own needs and direct our attention to the very One who promises to meet our needs.

Recently, I stumbled upon a "program of praise" developed by author Bob Hostetler.[1] It focuses on a different characteristic of God each day of the month. I have printed the list of godly attributes with the Bible verses that support them for each member of my family and have placed the list on their nightstands for easy access at bedtime. There is nothing more beautiful than praying Scripture aloud to God in the form of praise. Imagine if our daughters were to develop the habit (with or without our help) of praying each attribute to God on the designated day. Before long, the attributes of God would become so familiar to them that they would roll off their tongues as nuggets of truth embedded deep within their hearts. Just as we desire for someone to know and accept us for who we are, God desires the same from us. What better way to know Him than by giving Him the adoration He deserves on a daily basis.

Below is the "program of praise." See if it doesn't help you and your daughter further develop your adoration/praise of God.

1. God the Creator
   Creator God, I praise You because "you made the heavens, even the highest heavens, and all their starry host, the earth and all that is on it, the seas and all that is in them. You give life to everything, and the multitudes of heaven worship you" (Neh. 9:6).

2. The Only God

   God, I praise You because You are "the LORD, and there is no other; apart from [You] there is no God" (Isa. 45:5).

3. The Almighty God

   "O LORD God Almighty, who is like you? You are mighty, O LORD," and I praise you (Ps. 89:8).

4. The Everlasting Father, the Ancient of Days

   I praise You, Lord, as the "Ancient of Days" (Dan. 7:9), the "Everlasting Father" (Isa. 9:6) who lives forever and ever.

5. A Loving God

   I praise You because You are a loving God, whose very nature is love (1 John 4:16).

6. A God of Justice

   Lord, I praise and magnify You, who is just and the one who justifies those who have faith in Jesus (Rom. 3:26).

7. The Trustworthy God

   Heavenly Father, I give You my praise and adoration, because You are a "faithful God, keeping [Your] covenant of love to a thousand generations of those who love [You] and keep [Your] commands" (Deut. 7:9).

8. A Merciful God

   You, O Lord, "are a gracious and merciful God" (Neh. 9:31), and I praise you for your great mercy.

9. God My Refuge, My Fortress

   I praise you, Lord, for you are "my mighty rock, my refuge" (Ps. 62:7).

10. A Longsuffering, Persevering God

    Father, I praise You because You are "patient with [all Your children], not wanting anyone to perish, but everyone to come to repentance" (2 Pet. 3:9). Thank You for Your patience with me.

11. The Only Wise God
I give praise to You, my Father, "the only wise God [my] Saviour" (Jude 25 KJV). May all glory and majesty, dominion and power be Yours both now and ever.

12. The Holy One
"Holy, holy, holy [are You,] Lord God Almighty, who was, and is, and is to come" (Rev. 4:8).

13. A Personal God
I praise You, God, because You are a personal God, who gives me the honor of knowing You personally, just like You did to Abraham, Isaac, and Jacob (see Matt. 8:11).

14. A Giving God
Praise and honor be Yours, O God, because You are a generous God, who did not even stop short of giving Your own Son (see John 3:16).

15. The Provider God
I praise You today, Lord, as my Jehovah-jireh, who will generously provide all I need (see 2 Cor. 9:7).

16. The Shepherd God
I bless Your name and praise You as my Jehovah-rohi, who will shepherd me and guide me "in the paths of righteousness for [Your] name's sake" (Ps. 23:1–3).

17. God my Victory
Praise to You, my God, because You are my Jehovah-nissi, God my victory, "who always leads [me] in triumphal procession in Christ" (2 Cor. 2:14).

18. God my Peace
I praise You with all my heart, Lord, because You are my Jehovah-shalom, "the God of peace [who] will soon crush Satan under [my] feet" (Rom. 16:20).

19. The God Who Heals
"Father, I praise you because you are 'the LORD who heals [me]'" (Exod. 15:26).

20. The God of All Comfort
"Praise be to the God and Father of our Lord Jesus Christ, the Father of compassion and the God of all comfort" (2 Cor. 1:3).

21. The God of Miracles
Lord, I praise you because "You are the God who performs miracles; you display your power among the peoples" (Ps. 77:14).

22. A Forgiving God
I want to bless You with my praise, Father, because "you are a forgiving God, gracious and compassionate, slow to anger and abounding in love" (Neh. 9:17).

23. The Burden-Bearer
"Praise be to the LORD, to God [my] Savior, who daily bears [my] burdens" (Ps. 68:19).

24. A Faithful God
I praise You because "Your love, O LORD, reaches to the heavens, your faithfulness to the skies. . . . Great is your faithfulness" (Ps. 36:5; Lam. 3:23).

25. God the Blessed and Only Ruler, King of Kings and Lord of Lords
All honor and praise be to You, my "God, the blessed and only Ruler, the King of kings and Lord of lords" (1 Tim. 6:15).

26. God the Liberator
I praise you because "You are my help and my deliverer; O LORD" (Ps. 70:5).

27. The Lifter of My Head
Father God, I praise you because "you are a shield around me, O LORD;" You bestow glory on me and lift up my head when I am weary or depressed (Ps. 3:3).

28. A God of Light
I praise You, Lord, because You are my light and my salvation, and because You "know what lies in darkness, and light dwells with [you]" (Ps. 27:1; Dan. 2:22).

29. A God of Joy

I give You my praise, O Lord, because "you have granted [me] eternal blessings and made [me] glad with the joy of your presence" (Ps. 21:6).

30. The God Who Answers Prayer

I praise and honor You, Father, because You are a God who loves to answer prayer, and who begins to answer even before I begin to pray (see Isa. 65:24).

31. The God of All the Earth

I praise and adore you, Lord, as "the Holy One of Israel . . . [my] Redeemer . . . the God of all the earth" (Isa. 54:5).

Confession

The C of ACTS stands for confession. Confession is basically agreeing with God concerning our sin and feeling sorrow for our sin. Unless we think and feel the same way that God does about our sin, we will not repent (turn from our sin and turn back to God) (see 2 Cor. 7:10). When I get to the confession part of prayer time with my children, I encourage them to think of something *specific* that they may have done that day, rather than make a general sweeping statement (ex: "Lord, I confess that I was wrong when I spoke disrespectfully to my mom when she picked me up late from school" versus "Lord, I confess that sometimes I can be disrespectful to my parents"). If their confession involves a wrongdoing against another person, encourage them to make it right with the person by asking for forgiveness. Also, if you are taking turns going back and forth with the ACTS model, allow your daughter to hear you confess some specific sin that you committed that day. In doing so, you model to your daughter that we all (yes, even moms!) have sinned and fall short of the glory of God (see Rom. 3:23). Once your daughter becomes a Christian, she should be encouraged to take an inventory of her day and respond to conviction that the Holy Spirit may have placed upon her heart.

She may not always feel comfortable confessing her sins in your presence, so encourage her to continue her confession time alone after your prayer time together has ended.

When our daughters confess their sins on a daily basis and acknowledge God's forgiveness, it reminds them that sin is a serious matter in the eyes of God. In a world that preaches moral relativism, the discipline of confession will remind our daughters that there are absolute moral standards that dictate right and wrong, good and evil. However, we should be quick to assure our daughters that no sin is too big for the forgiveness of God. First John 1:9 promises that "if we confess our sins, [God] is faithful and just and will forgive us our sins and purify us from all unrighteousness." We must help our daughters recognize and respond properly to the pangs of conviction brought by the Holy Spirit over wrongdoing. We must equip them with the tools to acknowledge the conviction, confess their sins, and repent. If the habit of confession is developed early on in our daughters' lives, the chances increase that when they are older, they will rush to God's throne of grace in full confidence, knowing that they will receive His mercy and grace in their time of need (see Heb. 4:16).

Thanks

The *T* in ACTS stands for "thanks." When I think of the need to thank God, I am reminded of the ten lepers spoken of in Luke 17:12–18. They all cried out to Jesus to have pity on them and heal them. He responded to their cries and told them to "go, show yourselves to the priests" (v. 14), and then He healed them on their way. Unfortunately, only one bothered to return and thank Him. Jesus asked the man, "Were not all ten cleansed? Where are the other nine? Was no one found to return and give praise to God except this foreigner?" (vv. 17–18). Often, I am guilty, like the nine lepers, of failing to thank God for answered prayers.

One practical solution to this problem is to use a prayer journal. This can be done by using a blank notebook and dividing the pages into two columns. In one column, list your prayer requests, and in the other column, mark when and how the prayer was answered. When keeping a prayer journal, we are more likely to notice when God answers our prayers and offer Him the thanks He deserves.

As hard as it is to remember to thank God when He answers our prayers, it is even harder to thank Him when He answers, but not in a way we had hoped. Nonetheless, in 1 Thessalonians 5:18, God calls us to "give thanks in all circumstances." This is the mark of true Christian maturity.

God reminds us in Psalm 50:23 that "he who sacrifices thank offerings honors me." In addition to teaching our daughters to thank God for answered prayer, we should also teach our daughters to express thanks for things that they might otherwise take for granted. This would include the blessings of family, extended family, church family, a place to live, food to eat, freedom to worship, and the list goes on and on. Once again, if our daughters hear us express thanks to God for our many blessings, we model what it looks like to have a heart of gratitude.

One of the greatest benefits of regularly thanking God in our prayers is that expressing thanks to God is a strong antidote for discontentment. Discontentment results from focusing on the things we don't have or haven't achieved; giving thanks to God, however, gets our focus on the things we do have and have achieved. It is my desire to raise a daughter who doesn't just see the glass as half full, but recognizes that, thanks be to God, her cup runneth over.

Supplication

The *S* in ACTS stands for "supplication." Supplication is when we submit our requests or petitions to God on behalf of ourselves or others. As a reflection of the principle of putting others before ourselves, I am trying to develop the habit of submitting requests for others before I pray for myself. I have taught the same principle to my daughter.

If your daughter is young, do not be dismayed if her requests seem shallow. It may seem trivial when our daughters pray for things like the lizard who lost its tail, but they are at least getting the concept down of putting the needs of others (yes, lizards count) before their own needs. We can help them develop the habit of taking thought of others by gently asking them, "Is there anyone you would like to pray for tonight?" As they get older, they may want some privacy when they are praying for others or themselves. We should not take it personally, as our goal is to raise daughters who are comfortable conversing one-on-one with God. As your daughter begins to gain independence, you might say a quick prayer for her at bedtime and then leave her to pray alone. It is no different from other areas of training. The goal is to give our daughters a foundation for a healthy prayer life and assist them until they can master it on their own.

We must teach our daughters early on that God is the Father of compassion and the God of all comfort, who is capable of comforting them in all their troubles (see 2 Cor. 1:3–4). "Troubles" can range from an "owie" when they're two, a parent's divorce when they are ten, being left off the invitation list for a big party when they're thirteen, a breakup when they are seventeen, or anything, for that matter, that leads to tears or a broken heart. Girls who learn to run to Jesus in times of sadness or suffering are less likely to turn to other unhealthy things (food, alcohol, drugs, shopping, busyness, sex outside of marriage, etc.) when seeking comfort. As much as we desire to protect our daughters from hurtful situations in life, it will be impossible. While it is a wonderful thing if our daughters count us as trusted confidants when they are hurting, we need to be careful to show them comfort while at the same time pointing them in the direction of the only One who can mend a broken heart.

Hebrews 5:7 says, "During the days of Jesus' life on earth, he offered up prayers and petitions with loud cries and tears to the one who could save him from death, and he was heard because of his reverent submission." Because Jesus had submitted to His Father's authority even before His Father had answered His prayer, He was at peace regardless of the answer. Submission to God expressed through prayer says, "Your will be done," even if it is an answer that was not expected. If our daughters understand this concept, they will be less likely to question why God may choose not to answer some of their prayers in the ways that they hope. They will understand that "no" or "wait" is as valid an answer to their prayers as "yes."

Pray Without Ceasing

When I was a new believer, I remember experiencing some confusion over the call in 1 Thessalonians 5:17 to "pray without ceasing" (KJV). How does one pray constantly? The Greek word used for "without ceasing," is *adialeiptos*, which means "uninterruptedly." Since prayer is the way we communicate with God, and communicating with God is critical to our living as God desires, it only makes sense that we should be mindful of anything that would interrupt our communication with God. While I believe it is important to have a set time for prayer, it does not have to be relegated to that time. We must teach our daughters that God is accessible every minute of every day. When they develop the instinct to turn to God throughout their day, whether to lift up a request or a praise to Him, they will learn the art of what it is to pray without ceasing. Children, who develop the habit of taking thought of and talking to God throughout each day on their own initiative, are much less likely to fall into tempting situations or make foolish decisions when standing at the crossroads of a difficult choice.

One of the most difficult things for me when it comes to prayer is learning to stop and listen for the still, quiet voice of God. Sometimes in my morning prayer time, I spend moments in silence after going through the ACTS model. It is amazing the answers I have received when I've stopped talking to God and started listening to Him. I have encouraged my daughter to take time to listen carefully for God's voice.

> Be still, and know that I am God; I will be exalted among the nations, I will be exalted in the earth. (Ps. 46:10)

Praying for Our Daughters

While this chapter has focused on equipping our daughters with a heritage of prayer, it is equally important for us to exercise the privilege of praying for our daughters. Entire books have been devoted to the subject of mothers praying for their children. My husband and I consistently tell our children that we are praying for them. In addition to lifting them up in our personal prayer times, my husband has made it part of his morning routine to pray with and for my children at breakfast. He briefly describes character attributes that our children need to develop, and he prays for that attribute to be developed in their lives. He has been doing it for so long that my children can define the meaning of each attribute before my husband finishes reading the definition. If you don't have a list of character attributes that you define and pray with your children, consider using the one below.

31 Christian Attributes to Pray for Our Children[2]

1. Pray for a spirit of *humility*.
   The willingness to submit—James 4:10.
2. Pray for a spirit of *reverence*.
   The fear of the Lord—Proverbs 9:10.
3. Pray for a spirit of *purity*.
   A desire to be clean—Matthew 5:8.
4. Pray for a spirit of *purpose*.
   A wisdom to set goals—Proverbs 4:25.
5. Pray for a spirit of *simplicity*.
   A lifestyle uncluttered—Romans 12:8.

6. Pray for a spirit of *commitment*.
   A dedication to the "cause"—Joshua 24:15.
7. Pray for a spirit of *diligence*.
   A willingness to work hard—2 Peter 1:5.
8. Pray for a spirit of *servanthood*.
   The ministry of helps—Galatians 6:9–10.
9. Pray for a spirit of *consistency*.
   The quality of faithfulness—James 1:8.
10. Pray for a spirit of *assurance*.
    A depth of faith—Hebrews 10:22.
11. Pray for a spirit of *availability*.
    A willingness to go—Isaiah 6:8.
12. Pray for a spirit of *loyalty*.
    A zeal for fidelity—Ruth 1:16.
13. Pray for a spirit of *sensitivity*.
    Openness of heart—Luke 10:30–37.
14. Pray for a spirit of *compassion*.
    Love in action—Mark 8:1–2.
15. Pray for a spirit of *tenderness*.
    A willingness to weep—2 Kings 22:19.
16. Pray for a spirit of *maturity*.
    The capacity to grow—Hebrews 5:12–14.
17. Pray for a spirit of *holiness*.
    Christlike behavior—1 Peter 1:16.
18. Pray for a spirit of *reliability*.
    A depth of dependability—1 Corinthians 4:2.
19. Pray for a spirit of *revelation*.
    Learning to listen—Ephesians 1:15–18.
20. Pray for a spirit of *denial*.
    A sacrifice to surrender—Luke 9:23.
21. Pray for a spirit of *confidence*.
    A baptism of boldness—Philippians 4:13.
22. Pray for a spirit of *integrity*.
    The quality of truthfulness—Romans 12:17.

23. Pray for a spirit of *repentance*.
    A willingness to change—Luke 3:8.
24. Pray for a spirit of *trust*.
    A fearless reliance—Psalm 125:1.
25. Pray for a spirit of *submission*.
    Choosing to yield—Ephesians 5:21.
26. Pray for a spirit of *teachability*.
    A quality of meekness—Titus 3:2.
27. Pray for a spirit of *prayer*.
    A longing to wait—Isaiah 40:31.
28. Pray for a spirit of *unity*.
    A respect for others—1 Corinthians 1:10.
29. Pray for a spirit of *restoration*.
    A ministry of healing—Isaiah 61:1–2.
30. Pray for a spirit of *authority*.
    A capacity to command—Matthew 16:19.
31. Pray for a spirit of *generosity*.
    The desire to give—Matthew 10:8.

I realize that some mothers who are reading this may be experiencing a strained relationship with their daughters. If this is the case for you, suggest to your daughter that you pray aloud *with* her and *for* her once a week. Allow her to hear you thanking God for her. Since Paige was little, she has heard me pray: "Thank you God for picking me to be Paige's mother."

A dear friend of mine once mentioned in a speaking engagement that she developed the habit of praying for each of her children out loud in their respective rooms while they were at school. The first time I tried it, I ended up carrying a box of tissues with me from room to room. The experience moved me beyond words as I looked around their rooms, knowing that a day would come when their clothes would be picked up off the floor and their familiar knickknacks cleared off the shelves. I prayed aloud for each of them, their unique needs at their respective stages of life, their character development, and their future spouses should it be in God's will that they some-day marry. Most of all, I prayed that they would come to a place of utter dependence on Jesus Christ and claim Him for their very own. Someday, God willing, they too might stand in their children's bedrooms, tissues in hand, and verbally beseech the loving Father on behalf of their own children.

Questions for Individual Reflection or Group Study

1. Would you say that you have a healthy prayer life?
2. After reading about the ACTS model, is there an area of prayer to which you need to give more attention? If yes, which one(s) and why?
3. Have you been active in praying with your daughter? If yes, what model have you used? Has it been effective?
4. Do you run to the God of all comfort in times of sad-ness? Have you taught your daughter to do so?
5. Is it difficult for you to pray that "God's will be done" and accept the answer, even if it's not the one you wanted? Does your daughter understand this concept?
6. Do you "pray without ceasing"?
7. Are you in the habit of listening for God's still, quiet voice during your prayer times? Is your daughter?
8. Do you pray for your daughter on a regular and con-sistent basis? Does she know that she is prayed for by her mother?

CHAPTER TWELVE

A Heritage of Faith

> Common sense is not faith, and faith is not common
> sense; they stand in the relation of the natural and the
> spiritual; of impulse and inspiration. Nothing Jesus
> Christ ever said is common sense, it is revelation sense,
> and it reaches the shores where common sense fails.
> Faith must be tried before the reality of faith is actual.
> —OSWALD CHAMBERS[1]

*Y*ears ago, when my oldest son, Ryan, was three years old and my daughter, Paige, was one, we were in a Christian bookstore and stumbled across some Bible character action figures. They had David, complete with a miniature slingshot; Joseph, with a coat of many colors; Moses and the stone tablets, and many more. Ryan, true to his age, stood mesmerized in front of the display of pint-sized Bible heroes and insisted that I identify each and every one. When I got to the figurine of Jesus dressed simply in a cotton tunic, Ryan demanded in the hearing of every person in the store, "I have to have Jesus!" What mother could resist? Minutes later we left the store with the Jesus figurine.

Later that afternoon we headed to the pediatrician's office for Paige's yearly well-check. Knowing that she was due for shots, Ryan and I prayed for her on the way. After a long wait in the waiting room, a nurse finally called her name. As we followed the nurse down a long corridor, Ryan expressed concern over his sister's plight. I reminded him that we had prayed for her and that God had heard our prayer. Ryan, much to my shock, belted out, "Mommy, we left Jesus in the car! You have to go get Him so He can help Paige!" It was then that I realized my young son was experiencing some confusion over the action figure. The nurse, with furrowed eyebrows and a look of suspicion, ushered us into our designated room and quickly left. I explained to Ryan that the "Jesus" in the car was a toy, while the actual Jesus sits at the right hand of God the Father. Further, I emphasized that while we cannot see Jesus, His Spirit lives in the hearts of those who believe in Him. Clearly the concept of faith being "certain of what we do not see" (Heb. 11:1) was lost on my three-year-old.

One of the most important things we can leave our daughters is a heritage of faith. Probably the biggest determinant in whether we leave our daughters a heritage of faith is whether we, as mothers, model to them what having faith in Jesus looks like. One of my favorite definitions of faith is "belief in action." It is one thing to verbalize our belief in Christ to our daughters but quite another to act upon that belief. If a mother's actions and attitudes consistently contradict her expressed belief in Jesus, her daughter will receive a mixed message that faith in Christ is all talk and no action.

Are you modeling a sincere faith in Christ to your daughter? Are your actions and attitudes consistent with your expressed belief in Jesus? If not, your daughter could be left with the impression that faith in Christ is not a serious matter. Below are ten faith compromisers, which, if practiced consistently and modeled to your daughter, will prevent you from leaving her a true heritage of faith in Christ.

Top Ten Faith Compromisers

1. Not Attending Church Regularly

Consistent attendance at a Bible-believing church is essential for spiritual growth. Why is church attendance important? In a Bible-believing church, Christians learn the Bible and how to apply it to their lives, have an opportunity to fellowship with other believers, participate in corporate worship, and receive encouragement, accountability, and comfort.

When I was a Sunday school teacher years ago in the children's department, my heart was grieved over the children on my class roster who only attended Sunday school and church sporadically. While sporadic attendance was better than no attendance at all, the moms' and/or dads' unwillingness to make Sunday school and church a priority sent the clear message to their children that Sunday school and church attendance was not important.

I was also grieved over the number of parents who told me they stopped attending Sunday school or church because one or more of their children did not want to go. Given that logic, I wonder if they let their children miss school on days they would rather sleep in or watch their favorite cartoon. The spiritual foundation established by consistent church attendance will lend itself to a stronger and deeper faith in Jesus. My children know that Sunday school and church are only missed due to illness or vacation. As our children have gotten older, they are receiving more and more invitations to spend the night on Saturday nights. We rarely allow our children to have friends spend the night on Saturday nights or spend the night out with friends on Saturday night. We make occasional exceptions if the friend they wish to invite over does not attend church. On the rare occasions where they are allowed to spend the night out on Saturday nights, we expect them to go to bed at a reasonable hour and attend church the next morning with their friend. There is no reason that God should get the dregs of our lives on Sunday morning. He deserves our full attention, energy, and devotion. Just as we desire that our children go to bed at a reasonable hour on school nights so they are rested the next day, we should expect the same on "church nights" so they will be rested for Sunday school and church.

2. Worshipping Only on Sundays

Many Christians mistakenly assume that "worship" only means singing hymns or choruses on Sunday morning at church. In truth, Romans 12:1 tells us, "I urge you, brothers, in view of God's mercy, to offer your bodies as living sacrifices, holy and pleasing to God—this is your spiritual act of worship." It is God's desire that we offer ourselves to Him in worship on a continual basis, rather than one morning a week. Worship is a state of mind that acknowledges that God is holy and worthy of awe and reverence.

When Jesus encountered the Samaritan woman at the well, He informed her that the time had come when "true worshipers will worship the Father in spirit and truth, for they are the kind of worshipers the Father seeks" (John 4:23). True worshipers submit to the will and authority of God on a continual basis. Worship is much more than a sincere song offered to a Holy God on a Sunday morning. Worship says, "I love you." How do we show our love to God on a continual basis? Scripture tells us that God knows we love Him when we obey Him (see John 14:23). Worship is love for God expressed through consistent obedience. It will be impossible to offer ourselves to God as "living sacrifices" without obedience.

> Does the LORD delight in burnt offerings and sacrifices as much as in obeying the voice of the LORD? To obey is better than sacrifice.
> (1 Sam. 15:22a)

3. *Worrying or Failing to Trust God in Times of Adversity*

There is no greater peace in life than coming to a place where you can say, "Whatever, Lord. Your will be done." I am ashamed to say that in my nearly twenty-year walk with Christ, I have spent the majority of the years in the "freak out" mode when adversity hits. I had always admired Christians who appeared calm while in the eye of the storm and wondered if, perhaps, they didn't curl up in a fetal position behind closed doors. As I became more devoted to knowing God through His Word and prayer, I began to put my belief in Him into action. It is not that I don't experience an occasional moment of panic in times of uncertainty, but I can usually renew my mind in the Truth that has become embedded within my heart, which helps extinguish the onset of doubt.

Whether it is a loss of a job, the death of a loved one, a prodigal child gone astray, a broken marriage, or in my case, a child months shy of getting his driver's license, we can cast our cares on the Lord and He will sustain us (see Ps. 55:22).

In years past I struggled with a fear of flying. When God called me into a national speaking ministry, I faced a difficult dilemma. I could obey God's call and face my fear of flying, or I could run like Jonah and ignore (but not escape) God's call on my life. The first few flights were tough, but in no time I had mastered flying. Once I was strapped in my seat, I barely noticed when the plane took off or landed.

This calm peace lasted for years, until I experienced a flight that left me wondering if my days were up. Unfortunately, I was not alone—my daughter was with me. We were returning from a mother-daughter trip with seven other pairs of mothers and daughters. The mothers were sitting in the midsection of the plane, and our daughters, all ten to eleven years old, were in the rear of the plane. About halfway through the flight, we began to experience some turbulence.

From my experience as a traveler, it appeared to be nothing out of the ordinary. Nonetheless, some of our girls became scared and began calling from the back of the plane. The flight attendants had ordered everyone into their seats, and the seat belt light was turned on. The mothers knew that there was one empty seat beside our girls, and I volunteered to make my way to the back of the plane to sit with the girls in an attempt to calm their fears. I knew it must be serious when on my way back, the flight attendants began screaming at me to hurry and take a seat. I also couldn't help but notice that they were not sitting in their jump seats, but were scattered throughout the plane in some of the available coach seats. I quickly made it to the seat across from the girls and buckled my seat belt.

No sooner had I snapped my seat belt than the plane went into what appeared to be a free fall. After what seemed like an eternity, the plane made a hard lean to the right. Some people screamed as the plane jolted. The girls were crying, and one said, "Mrs. Courtney, are we going to die?" Fortunately, the Holy Spirit took over, and to my surprise, words of comfort began to flow from my mouth. It's a good thing because I wanted to scream, *"I want my mommy!"* My worst fear was being realized, but rather than scribble my last will and testament on the drink napkin, I suggested to the girls that we pray. As I was praying for our safety, a Bible verse came to mind, and without thinking, I prayed, "Father we know that you are watching over us and that Scripture tells us 'not even a sparrow will fall to the ground apart from your will.'" While this verse had always brought comfort to me (on the ground), it somehow caused the girls to cry even louder, not to mention, a few passengers sitting nearby! Within minutes the plane seemed to correct itself, and we safely landed. I knew this was not your standard bout of turbulence when I witnessed a couple of the flight attendants crying and consoling each other!

Today that flight is a faded memory, and the girls and moms laugh at the thought of Mrs. Courtney's "comforting" prayer. I have flown on many flights since then, and when turbulence hits, I bow my head and silently pray, "Whatever, Lord, Your will be done."

> But blessed is the man who trusts in the LORD, whose confidence is in him. He will be like a tree planted by the water that sends out its roots by the stream. It does not fear when heat comes; its leaves are always green. It has no worries in a year of drought and never fails to bear fruit. (Jer. 17:7–8)

4. Failing to Put Your Money Where Your Mouth Is

A recent Barna Research survey found that only 6 percent of born-again Christian households tithed to their churches in 2002.[2] Malachi 3:10 instructs us to "'bring the whole tithe into the storehouse, that there may be food in my house. Test me in this,' says the LORD Almighty, 'and see if I will not throw open the floodgates of heaven and pour out so much blessing that you will not have room enough for it.'" A tithe is defined as one-tenth of our earnings. In giving a tenth of our income back to God, we acknowledge that 100 percent of all we have belongs to God, and without Him, we would have nothing.

Why is a failure to tithe a faith compromiser? If one claims to believe wholeheartedly in Christ and the commandments set forth in God's Word, he/she should be willing to entrust to God a portion (10 percent or more) of what rightly belongs to Him in the first place. Regardless of whether a Christian's failure to tithe is due to a real or perceived lack of finances or simply a preference to spend the money elsewhere, failure to tithe shows a lack of trust in God. If one cannot trust God with their finances, they will struggle to trust Him in other areas of life as well.

Who can forget the widow's gift of two copper coins that caught the eye of Jesus? He noted that while the others gave their gifts out of their wealth, the widow gave out of her poverty. It is not the amount of one's gift that matters to God, but the act of obedience in giving, one's attitude in giving, and the level of sacrifice.

As mothers, we must model the discipline of tithing to our children and train them to tithe their allowance or other income. Children who grow up tithing 10 percent of their earnings are much more likely to tithe in their adult years. I have told my daughter that she should not even consider marrying a man who compromises in the area of tithing. In doing so, he shows a lack of faith in God that will not be limited to his finances. If he can dismiss God's command to tithe when it becomes difficult to do so, what keeps him from dismissing the command to remain faithful in marriage whenever the marriage gets difficult?

God's command in Malachi to bring our tithes to the storehouse is preceded by a reprimand that the people were robbing God of His tithes. Our children must be taught that in addition to demonstrating a lack of faith in God, one's decision not to tithe is a decision to rob God of what rightly belongs to Him.

After becoming a Christian in my college years, I recall the first time I heard my pastor preach on tithing. I had never even heard the word and had no idea what it meant. When the pastor explained the purpose of the tithe, a light-bulb went off in my head. I had never stopped to think about how the church paid its bills, salaries, and daily operational costs. We must teach our children that God's tithe goes to support the local church as well as outreach and mission efforts.

When my husband and I were newly married and in the market for a new home, we met with a real estate agent. We were not sure of the price range of house we could afford, so the agent assisted us in calculating what price of home we could qualify to purchase based on our salary and monthly expenses. When my husband got to the amount we paid monthly in a tithe to our church, the agent was stunned and asked if it was negotiable. She explained that we could afford a much nicer home if we were willing to give up the tithe amount and put it toward the house payment. We walked out of her office and never looked back. What a shame that she did not realize that we would be far more blessed in giving our tithes to God than living in a home with a few hundred more square feet.

5. Being a Whiner

If you want to send a mixed message to your daughter, tell her that she can have an abundant and content life if she will allow Jesus to be the Lord of her life—but then whine and complain in front of her all the time. If you desire that your daughter adopt your Christian faith and experience the abundant life that Christ referred to in John 10:10, she must witness that your faith in Christ has resulted in the abundant life. Faith in Christ should bring a new attitude fueled by an overwhelming sense of gratefulness to Him.

No doubt, we all experience a good whine from time to time. The problem arises if we are chronic whiners. Chronic whiners can hardly carry on a conversation without saying something that is negative or critical in nature. Chronic whiners today are no different from the Israelite whiners in the wilderness that are described in the Old Testament. They grumbled and complained from the onset of their miraculous deliverance by God from Egypt until their entrance into the promised land forty years later. Similarly, chronic whiners today easily forget their deliverance through Christ from the slavery of sin and choose to wallow in the wilderness of grumbling and complaining. Their negative and critical spirit negates any lip service they have given to the benefits of being a Christian, *especially* if they whine often about spiritual matters. Oftentimes, if you trace church divisions to their origins, you will find one or more chronic whiners at the source of the conflict.

The root of whining is discontentment, and discontentment is always a choice. The root of discontentment is ungratefulness to, and lack of faith in, God. If you find yourself being discontent, a very practical way to address it is to make a mental or physical list of all you have to be thankful for. Another great antidote to discontentment is to study Philippians 4:10–19, where Paul discusses contentment.

Our daughters are watching and *listening*. If we are whining mothers, we will almost certainly raise whining daughters, who will someday grow up to be whining mothers. We need to teach our daughters that too much "whine" can be hazardous to their spiritual health.

6. *Not Sharing Your Faith with Others*

A person's final words are always of importance. In Jesus' final words before He died, He could have emphasized the importance of loving our neighbors or giving to the poor, but instead He exhorted believers to "go and make disciples of all nations, baptizing them in the name of the Father and of the Son and of the Holy Spirit, and teaching them to obey everything I have commanded you" (Matt. 28:19–20). Jesus was not making a mere suggestion to tell others about Him and the good news of the gospel; He was making a commandment.

We minimize the importance of faith in Jesus Christ if we teach our daughters that a personal relationship with God through Jesus Christ is the most important thing in life yet fail to share the gospel of Jesus with others. It sends a message that we are only concerned with our own salvation. In 1 Corinthians 9:16, Paul said, "Yet when I preach the gospel, I cannot boast, for I am compelled to preach. Woe to me if I do not preach the gospel!" As recipients of the life-changing power of the gospel message, we too should be compelled to tell others about the gospel of Jesus. As mothers, we need to teach our daughters this truth by our words and, most importantly, our lifestyles.

7. Molding Your Faith to Fit Your Life Rather Than Molding Your Life to Fit Your Faith

Many Christians treat their faith as an afterthought or minor detail in the scheme of their lives. Their belief in Christ is merely one of many aspects that influence their lives, rather than being the preeminent, foundational aspect of their lives.

We all can probably think of times we were shocked when someone told us he was a Christian because his life did not support it. I can't help but think of Peter, who denied Christ three times after declaring to Him, "Even if all fall away on account of you, I never will" (Matt. 26:33). Peter discovered the hard way that believing in Christ is not always easy. When the rubber hit the road, he chose safety over following Jesus. Peter faced a crisis of belief. Was Jesus who He claimed to be? In the end, Peter did determine that, indeed, Jesus was the Messiah, the Son of the living God. By the time he proclaimed Christ to thousands on the day of Pentecost, Peter had remolded his life to fit his faith. He was transformed from a "closet Christian" to one of the boldest and most vocal disciples of Christ ever known.

Would those who know you be shocked to discover that you are a Christian? Would people be able to identify you as a faithful follower of Christ after spending time with you? If not, you run the risk of leaving your daughter a heritage of watered-down faith. If this is the case, she may conclude that *Christian* is merely a label rather than a lifestyle. The only way to prevent this is to develop your life around your faith in Jesus rather than attempt to make your faith fit comfortably into your life.

8. Failing to Put Your Past in Its Place

After years of ministering to women, I have determined that one of the greatest hindrances to women growing into mature, faithful Christians is their failure to put their past in its place. I often tell women in my speaking engagements that Satan's greatest desire is to be granted their souls for all eternity. Once a woman becomes a Christian, she is out of Satan's reach for eternity. At that point he moves to Plan B, which is to try to cause her to doubt that she has been saved from her sins and is a child of God. He will do everything in his power to burden her with shame and false guilt over her past. A failure adequately to understand God's grace and forgiveness will hinder her from sharing the power of the cross with others.

I know firsthand the toll that shame and guilt over the past can take on your spiritual life. When the skeletons in my closet began to tumble out, I had a hard time believing that God could actually forgive me for some of the things I had done. Somewhere in the midst of my guilt trip, the Holy Spirit convicted my heart that by failing to accept that all my sins had been forgiven, I was minimizing the death of my Savior on the cross. Forgiveness of our sins came with a tremendous price. God's desire is that we respond with gratitude and be forever changed. If you feel shame over your past, Satan is getting the victory.

One of the most common questions I get when doing events for mothers and daughters is, "How much do I tell my daughter about my past?" There is no absolute answer to this question, but I tell mothers to spend some time praying about it first. I caution them to check their motives and make sure they are sharing for the right reasons. If they are sharing mistakes from their past to receive comfort from their daughters, they are sharing for the wrong motives. It is inappropriate for us to place a burden on our daughters to meet our emotional needs or to heal our past hurts. Sharing mistakes from our pasts should be for the purpose of illustrating our regret for past sin and the power of God's forgiveness, nothing more. Also, I caution mothers that it should be age appropriate and to avoid specifics if they are led to share. They should avoid sharing details that serve little or no purpose.

As much as we desire to protect our daughters from falling into some of the same temptations and sins we may have experienced, it is impossible to keep our thumbs on them every minute of every day. They too will commit sins along the way and find themselves in need of a loving, forgiving Savior. If you are hesitant to share some of your past mistakes with your daughter at times when it would be appropriate, ask yourself why. If you are overwhelmed with shame, it could be that the enemy (Satan) has done a number on you. Don't allow him the opportunity to hold you in bondage to your past any longer. If you have, by faith, received Jesus as your Savior, He has set you free from the spiritual consequences and bondage of your sins. If your daughter witnesses a mother whose heart is overwhelmed with gratitude at the mere thought of the cross, your daughter will have a better understanding of God's grace. She will also know that it came with a heavy price.

9. Being Prideful and Legalistic

One morning, while reading the newspaper, I ran across a story on the front page about several college women from the University of Texas who had modeled nude for an edition of *Playboy* magazine that featured college women from across the country. My heart was saddened when I read that one of the girls was a pastor's daughter, a past member of the Fellowship of Christian Athletes in high school, and had been very involved in her church youth group. In the article she claimed that "her faith was no longer important to her."

Out of curiosity I e-mailed her the following day and politely asked her if she would be willing to share with me the factors that led her to conclude that her faith was no longer important. Her response was far from kind, to say the very least, but in between her excessive use of profanities, she indicated that her father had been a primary factor. She said that he was harsh, unloving, critical, and legalistic. Nothing she could ever do was good enough in his eyes. She said he knew the Bible backward and forward and had quoted verses to her on a daily basis since the time she was young. In high school she did not drink, smoke, date, or curse, and she attended church every time the doors opened, but she claimed that it still was not enough to satisfy her father. When she got to college, she let loose. It was the classic tale of good girl gone bad. While my gut told me that there was another side to this sad story, I couldn't help but wonder if this young lady's words didn't have a ring of truth to them. As mothers, we would be wise to remember that "rules without relationship equals rebellion."[3] Jesus had harsh words for the Pharisees in Scripture who were legalistic and nitpicked over the letter of the law, using it primarily to pass judgment on everyone but themselves. Worst of all, they did so absent of the love of God.

If I have a faith that can move mountains, but have not love, I am nothing. (1 Cor. 13:2b)

10. Failing to Have a Daily Quiet Time

It will be impossible to pass down a heritage of faith to our daughters unless we consistently set aside time for prayer and reading God's Word. So important are both these factors that they merited their own chapters in this book (chapters 10 and 11). The more we talk to God in prayer and the more we get to know Him through His Word, the deeper our faith in Him. Daughters who witness mothers who have consistent prayer lives and depend on His Word (the Bible) for their daily sustenance will witness, firsthand, belief in action.

I can think of no better way to end this book than a chapter devoted to leaving a heritage of faith. If there was ever a person who could attest to the benefits of being left a heritage of faith, it is I. Long before I ever came to know Christ, I was blessed with two sets of godly grandparents who were committed to praying for my lost soul. Their persistence paid off when I came to know Christ in my college years. Since that time, I have been blessed with children of my own, and I have witnessed each one come to know Christ as their personal Savior. Years ago I watched my mother return to her own godly heritage of faith upon being diagnosed with a brain tumor. The tumor was benign and the surgery was a success. As of late, I have watched her desperately cling to the promises in God's Word as her marriage of forty years to my father unexpectedly ended in divorce. She finds solace in the knowledge that she is not alone, for God will be her husband. She is an inspiration to me and proof that it is never too late to come home to God. As I look at the four generations of mothers and daughters in my family, I am struck by the fact that we have each traveled very different spiritual journeys. Yet, in the end, we share the same bond of faith in Jesus Christ. It is our heritage.

My daughter has been given a great godly heritage, and so has yours. How do I know that? Because you cared enough to read this book, and that speaks volumes about the importance you place on your call as a mother. We as mothers can do our part in passing down the torch of a godly heritage, but in the end, it will be up to our daughters to decide whether they will carry the torch and, in turn, pass it down to their own children. Let us rest in the hope of Proverbs 22:6: "Train a child in the way he should go, and when he is old he will not turn from it."

Questions for Individual Reflection or Group Study

1. Look over the list of the Top Ten Faith Compromisers. Were there any that struck your heart with conviction? If so, which ones and why?
2. Does your family faithfully attend church? Does your family faithfully tithe 10 percent of its income to

your church? Do you feel that it is important to train your children to tithe?

3. What are some ways that you worship God throughout the week? Is your worship consistent? Does your worship include being a "living sacrifice" (obedient) to God?

4. How do you respond in times of adversity—ignore God, blame God, or look to God for help?

5. Has your daughter ever witnessed you sharing your faith with others?

6. Overall, would you say that you have molded your life to fit your faith or molded your faith to fit your life?

7. Have you put your past in its place? How do you feel about sharing some of your past mistakes (at the right time) with your daughter as teachable moments (as God leads)?

8. Are you raising your daughter to be His girl?

Conclusion

pon completing a book, most authors feel a natural sense of relief and closure. "Relief" and "closure" are not words that describe what I am feeling as I write the final words of this book. An eternal optimist by nature, I am normally not one to play the role of the naysayer, but the disturbing facts regarding our present culture are hard to ignore. One need only turn on the television, flip through the fashion magazines, or observe the girls at the local teen hangout to witness the devastating fallout of a culture absent of biblical virtue. Some may argue that decadent and immoral influences have impacted culture in times past (the roaring 20s) and in the end proved to be nothing more than a passing phase. I fear this is different. In the past the majority voice represented the majority consensus that as a whole esteemed virtue and morality. Right was right and wrong was wrong. Immoral living was not tolerated, and it was only a matter of time before the majority consensus prevailed. Today virtue and morality are all but forgotten words. While surveys show that Christians are the majority in this country, we seem to have a minority voice when it comes to influencing culture. Many have been bullied into a prevailing sense of silence for fear of being labeled politically incorrect or intolerant. As a result, we are facing a moral free fall of epic proportion.

As mothers, we have our work cut out for us as we strive to raise godly daughters in an ungodly world. This reality became soberly clear as I was preparing for an upcoming message. I was thumbing through my stash of teen fashion magazines from the 1950s and 2000s to find fresh examples that would illustrate the changes young women have experienced over the last fifty years. Images of girls and boys sitting on the floor playing records, running through a field flying kites, and sipping sodas at the malt shop filled the pages of the early magazines. The articles highlighted family, friendships, patriotism, and surprisingly, an appreciation for good literature and art.

Fast-forward fifty years. Many of the partially clothed teen models appear harsh and rebellious. The charming, innocent smiles that came standard with the 1950s teen models are replaced with pouting come-and-get-it looks. Pants and jackets are partially unzipped, leaving little to the imagination. In the coed photos, the girls are usually portrayed as the aggressors, sending a clear message that girl power is no longer about equality but rather dominance and superiority.

Gone from the magazines are the articles highlighting art and literature. Who needs culture when you can read about such realities as a transgender teen girl who claims she is a male born into a female body? The reader is given graphic details about her partial sex change operation and subjected to a picture of this "young lady" showing the results from the waist up. She (referred to as "he" in the magazine) went into even more graphic detail when describing her sex life. Let me remind you that the magazine's target audience is girls ages twelve to seventeen. The article has left its indelible mark etched forever in my mind, and I can only imagine the harm it has done to its intended much younger audience. Another issue of the same magazine features "Love Stories," and shows two girls kissing. You won't find encouragement for modesty, virginity, or morality in these pages. Much of what I found was too shocking to share in a speaking message to teen girls.

Couple this with an abundance of sitcoms glamorizing sex outside of marriage and commercials that use sensuality to sell everything from shampoo to potato chips. We live in a culture where male rappers who sing degrading lyrics about women are rewarded with increased record sales. The MTV awards show will forever be remembered for the now-famous Britney-Madonna open-mouthed kiss. Madonna has been vocal in saying that she is "bored with the concept of right and wrong." How do we reward her behavior and resulting gibberish regarding moral relativism? We put the children's book she released weeks later on the *New York Times'* best-seller list! Where are the role models for our daughters? Can it get any worse than this? I fear it can.

After sharing a challenging message that focused on the current times and the resulting need to counteract the culture, I was approached by a mother. She thanked me for my ministry to young women and asked me if I ever get discouraged that the cry for change might just be a "ripple on the pond." I was initially taken aback as I pictured in my mind a ripple that quickly disappears on the surface of a pond. For days I pondered her words and wondered if perhaps she wasn't right. Is it hopeless? Do my meager efforts even matter? Before I could sink into the proverbial pity party, a new image entered my mind. Gone was the wimpy ripple on the pond, and in its place was a roaring ocean wave crashing on the sandy shore, stirring up everything in its path.

Days later, out of curiosity, I looked up the origin of waves. I was amazed to discover that the waves that break on the beach are created by wind blowing over the water. As the waves travel away from the area where they were initially generated in the open ocean, they evolve into long, smooth-crested waves called "swell waves." Swell waves can travel for very long distances across the ocean without losing the energy they acquired from the wind.

Upon making this discovery that waves were initiated by wind, I was immediately reminded of Ephesians 3:16 which says, *"I pray that out of his glorious riches he may strengthen you with power through his Spirit in your inner being."* I recalled that the Greek word for "Spirit" is "pneuma." When I looked it up, I was filled with hope. "Pneuma" means "current of air" or "breeze" initiated by something that is "superhuman" or "divine." In our own strength, we can produce nothing more than a ripple, but with God's help, through the Holy Spirit, what started as a ripple can someday become a wave.

> Heavenly Father, take my meager efforts, this book included, and make them more than just a ripple on a pond. Give my sisters and me the strength and wisdom needed to raise our daughters to be godly. Give us the boldness to make waves when it comes to the culture. Thank you for blessing us with daughters. May we be faithful in raising them to know that above all, they are Your girls.

Appendix: A Note to Mothers with Sons

*A*s the mother of two sons, I realize that my husband and I have a tremendous responsibility to raise our sons to respect young women in the way God intended. This chapter is written to challenge mothers to set the bar high when it comes to teaching their sons to respect women. Regardless of your son's age, it is never too early to teach him to respect the opposite sex.

Beauty Is More Than Skin Deep

In a culture that implies that women are nothing more than objects for the sexual gratification of men, it is difficult to teach our sons to look past what is on the outside and see the heart that lies beneath. In a culture laden with sensuality, our teenage boys will battle hormones in overdrive. Unfortunately, we cannot completely protect our sons from the sensuality and sexual references in advertisements, commercials, television programs, movies, and song lyrics. We can, however, teach them a proper response by revealing the lie of the culture that says "appearance is everything." We must remind them that each person is a precious creation of God, made in His likeness and image. Our sons are just as susceptible to buying into the world's equations for worth (see chap. 5) as our daughters. It might be a good idea to go over the worth equations with them in order to give them a basic understanding of the root cause of falsely defined worth.

One of the girls in my office, who is in her mid-twenties, shared a common frustration she and her single friends experience regarding some of the Christian guys in their singles group at church. The guys often speak openly about certain women being "hot," and they go into detail when describing specific physical attributes they find attractive in women. What would God say about adult Christian men engaged in locker room talk and, of all things, in the presence of their Christian sisters?

When I speak to college women, they echo my coworker's comments concerning the tendency among many Christian college men to view women as objects and treat them in a disrespectful manner. They say the playing field is short on good Christian guys who have been raised to honor and respect women. I fear that many Christian parents have rationalized that "boys will be boys" and have dismissed this disturbing behavior as a battle not worth fighting. Do these parents not realize that this type of behavior is a launching ground for more serious offenses, such as lust, fornication, adultery, and pornography? I warn college women to run fast and far from Christian men who show an unhealthy preoccupation toward outward appearance and obsess openly over physical attributes they find attractive in women. Their habits won't disappear with marriage.

Men and teenage boys who are in the habit of viewing women as objects are more likely to struggle with a chronic habit of lust and possibly even pornography. While it is no secret that many young women dress in such a way as to invite lust, it does not excuse the behavior. Proverbs 6:25–26 warns: "Do not lust in your heart after her beauty or let her captivate you with her eyes, for the prostitute reduces you to a loaf of bread, and the adulteress preys upon your very life."

Interestingly, the remedy prescribed to prevent such lust can be found in the five verses leading up to the warning. In a nutshell, the remedy is based on a "father's commands" and a "mother's teaching."

> My son, keep your father's commands and do
> not forsake your mother's teaching. Bind them upon
> your heart forever; fasten them around your neck.
> When you walk, they will guide you; when you sleep,
> they will watch over you; when you awake, they will
> speak to you. For these commands are a lamp, this
> teaching is a light, and the corrections of discipline
> are the way to life, keeping you from the immoral
> woman, from the smooth tongue of the wayward
> wife. (Prov. 6:20–24)

It is unrealistic to expect that our sons would not experience an initial attraction to girls based on their outward appearance since boys (and men) are wired internally to be stimulated visually. Keeping this in mind, it is important that we teach our sons that true beauty is more than just skin deep. Often, this is hard to do. I have had to catch myself many times from making comments to my son about girls being "cute" or "pretty," rather than emphasizing their character qualities. Sometimes I don't even realize I am doing the very thing I warn against! It is especially important that our sons hear us extolling attributes of Christianity that we notice in others: "She has a heart for Christ and it shows in the way she treats others." "She is so faithful to invite her school friends to church." "She dresses stylishly, yet modestly." As our sons hear us compliment girls in matters of Christian character and faith, they will be more likely to do so themselves and view women (and others) as whole persons.

Even with our teaching and modeling, given the current immodest clothes that girls wear, it is difficult for our sons to resist seeing girls (and women) as objects. Christian girls who choose to dress immodestly make it very difficult for their Christian brothers to remain pure in their thoughts and attitudes toward them, much less have respect for them. As a result of this problem, I read where a large group of Mormon boys developed and signed a "Modesty Proclamation" and presented it to the girls in their group. It basically asks the girls to consider the effect immodest attire has on boys and asks them to show "respect" to the boys by not putting them in a difficult and tempting situation. How I would love to see this happen in every church youth group across America! Let it start with mine!

We cannot monitor our sons' behavior twenty-four hours a day, seven days a week, to ensure that they properly view young women in the "whole person" category rather than the "object" category, but we can do our part to make sure they receive their "mothers' teaching." I have told my son, Ryan, that God has given him everything he needs to resist the temptation to view girls as objects, regardless of the influence of the culture. It is my prayer that I will raise sons who will see girls (and women) through God's eyes as being fearfully and wonderfully made both on the inside and the outside.

What Ever Happened to Old-Fashioned Chivalry?

If the *Titanic* were to sink today, only a little more than a third of men would give up their spots on the lifeboats to women outside of their immediate families. This is according to Pittsburgh *Post-Gazette's* "*Titanic* Test," where two hundred men were interviewed.[1] This should come as a relief to many feminists who have long scorned the preferential treatment gentlemen have historically extended to women in the name of good manners and chivalry. How ironic that they find disrespect to be an indicator of respect. On a recent flight, while wrestling to get my bag in the overhead bin, a nice gentleman came to the rescue. He kindly asked if he could help, and of course, I welcomed his assistance. I thanked him for being one of a dying breed of gentlemen (just loud enough for the other male cads who had remained seated). He commented that he had been trained from an early age to be courteous and extend a hand to women in need. He shared that, at times, women have smirked at him for opening a door or offering his seat. I wonder if these same women would smirk at him if he were to offer them his seat on a lifeboat while on the deck of a sinking ship. Somehow I doubt it.

Chivalry is a word that sparks imagery of the Middle Ages and the days of wandering knights. It was a point of honor for knights to protect others, even at the cost of personal hardship. Respect for women was an important part of the knight's code and formed a basis for many of the rules of politeness in our culture today. Unfortunately, those rules are not always followed.

At a recent visit to the orthodontist, my daughter and I walked in to find the waiting area full. We were about to take a seat on the floor when a man got up and signaled his two teenage sons to follow his lead and offer their seats to us. I thanked him profusely and overheard him talking to his sons about becoming more aware of situations when women are in need of a seat. It reminded me of our family trip to Disney World and a bus ride back to our hotel at the end of a long day. We had been on our feet most of the day and were relieved finally to have the opportunity to sit for an extended period of time. After several stops, the bus had filled up and my husband, being a gentleman, gave his seat to a woman who would otherwise have had to stand in the middle aisle and hang on to a bar above her head. He nodded for my oldest son, Ryan, to do the same, and he quickly complied. (I made a note to check his forehead for fever). Even so, there were not enough seats, and several children in the aisle were getting tossed about as they tried to hang on to their parents' legs. I was amazed at the number of young men who remained seated, fully aware of the circumstances. Finally, I stood up and offered a couple of small children my seat and told my daughter to do the same. She started to give me the "I'm a princess look" but thought better of it. I was teaching her that manners cross gender lines in the name of common courtesy.

There is no arguing that the single greatest influence in our sons' lives will be their fathers. Sons who witness fathers treating their mothers with respect will, most likely, grow up to be husbands who treat their wives with respect. I am fortunate to have a husband who models to our sons what it looks like to be a gentleman and a protector. He expects our sons to treat both me and my daughter with respect and courtesy. In addition, my boys have had the benefit of attending a Christian school where manners are taught and enforced. Boys are expected to fall back in line and allow the girls to go first when walking down the corridors. They are expected to hold the doors open for the girls.

Yet in spite of my sons' training, they have a long way to go. Just recently, when walking into a shopping center, my fifteen-year-old son walked ahead of me through the doors and failed to hold the door open for me. In order to teach him a lesson, I allowed the door to fold in on my body. He finally turned around and rushed back (laughing) to open the door. My stunt worked, and now he rushes to hold the door open for me, lest he risk public embarrassment. When in doubt, resort to public shaming! Our goal should be that by the time our boys leave the nest, they will be polite young men who exhibit manners to women, extend a hand to women in need, and respect women as whole persons rather than objects.

If you are a single mother or you are in a situation where your husband is not a good role model when it comes to training your son(s) about manners, do not despair. Although it will be difficult at times to carry the burden of training alone, it is not impossible. Your efforts will be well worth it in the end.

Endnotes

Chapter One: I Am Mother; Hear Me Roar!

1. "Number, Timing, and Duration of Marriages and Divorces: 1996," US Census Bureau, February 2000.

2. "Born Again Adults Less Likely to Co-Habit, Just as Likely to Divorce." Barna Research Group, press release, 6 August 2001.

3. Sara McLanahan and Gary Sandefur, *Growing Up with a Single Parent: What Hurts, What Helps* (Cambridge: Harvard University Press, 1994), 2.

4. "Breakdown on Family Breakdown," *The Washington Times*, 25 March 2001, B2.

5. Barbara Kantrowitz and Pat Klingert, "Unmarried, with Children," *Newsweek*, 28 May 2001, 46.

6. Eric Schmitt, "For First Time, Nuclear Families Drop Below 25 Percent of Households," *The New York Times*, 15 May 2001, A1.

7. Lydia Saad, "Moderate Drinking on the Rise," Gallup News Service, 19 September 2003.

8. "The NetValue Report on Minors Online," *Business Wire*, 19 December 2000.

9. "Alexa Research Finds 'Sex' Popular on the Web" *Business Wire*, 14 February 2001.

10. Kerby Anderson and Perry Brown, "The Peril of Pornography," American Tract Society.

11. "Sex on TV: Content and Context," Kaiser Family Foundation, 1999.

12. Jean Holzgang, "Facts on Body and Image," 14 April 2000, Just Think Foundation (http://www.justthink.org/bipfact.html).

13. "Media's Effect on Girls: Body Image and Gender Identity," National Institute on Media and the Family, 2002 (http://www.medi-afamily.org/facts/facts_mediaeffect.shtml).

14. "America's Children: Key National Indicators of Well-Being, 2001." Forum on Child and Family Statistics, 40 (http://www.child-stats.gov/ac2001/ac01.asp).

15. Ibid.

16. Youth Risk Behavior Surveillance System, Centers for Disease Control and Prevention, 2002.

17. "Teenage Sexual and Reproductive Behavior in the United States," Kaiser Family Foundation, 1997.

18. S. K. Henshaw, "U.S. Teenage Pregnancy Statistics with Comparative Statistics for Women Aged 20–24." The Alan Guttmacher Institute, 2003.

19. Foxnews.com, "Fast Facts: U.S. Abortion Statistics," 17 June 2003 (The article cites that sources are Planned Parenthood, National Center for Health Statistics.) (http://www.foxnews.com/story/0,2933,880,00.html).

20. "Americans Are Most Likely to Base Truth on Feelings," Barna Research Group, press release, 12 February 2002.

21. Independent Women's Forum Study, "Hooking Up, Hanging Out, and Hoping for Mr. Right."

22. Gloria Steinem quote (second-hand reports) (http://archive.salon.com/mwt/feature/1998/03/27feature.html).

23. Judith Hennessee, *Betty Friedan: Her Life* (New York: Random House, 1999).

24. "Women Warned of Infertility Trap," 11 April 2002 (http://www.CNN.com/Health).

25. *Seventeen*, April 1960.

26. *Seventeen*, May 1960, 75.

27. *Seventeen*, April 1970, 9.

28. *Seventeen*, 1950.

29. *Seventeen*, 1960, 145.

30. *Seventeen*, April 1960, 146.

31. *Ladies' Home Journal*, December 1948, 44–45.

32. *Seventeen*, December 2001, 174–78; excerpt from Margo Rabb's novel, *Missing Persons* (to be published in 2003 by Penguin).

33. "Facts & Stats-9," The National Campaign to Prevent Teen Pregnancy, 2002.

34. Eleanor Roosevelt, "If You Ask Me," *Ladies Home Journal*, December 1948, 40.

Chapter Two: Motherhood: A High Calling

1. Henry G. Bosch, "Mother's Influence," *Our Daily Bread*, 27 April 1996.
2. John Quincy Adams quote.
3. Barna Research Online (http://www.barna.org/cgi-bin/PagePressRelease.asp?PressReleaseID=117&Reference=F).
4. The Next American Spirituality/George Gallup Jr.
5. Barna Research Online.
6. George Barna, *Real Teens*, 2001.
7. Lynn Okagaki, in Shelvia Dancy, "You've Got to Spell It for Kids," 12 August 2000 (http://www.beliefnet.com/story/36/story_3672_1.html).
8. Gary Lyle Railsback, "An Exploratory Study of the Religiosity and Related Outcomes among College Students," Doctoral dissertation, University of California at Los Angeles, 1994.

Chapter Three: Counteracting the Culture

1. George Barna, *Real Teens*.
2. Ibid.
3. Ibid.

Chapter Four: The Dangers of Conformity

1. Misty Bernall, *She Said Yes* (New York: Pocket Books, 2000).
2. George Barna, *Real Teens*.
3. Alloy (http://www.alloy.com).
4. Ibid.
5. Josh McDowell, *Beyond Belief to Convictions* (Carol Stream, Ill.: Tyndale, 2002).
6. Ibid.
7. Nehemiah Institute; online article: One More Generation and then the End (http://www.nehemiahinstitute.org).

Chapter Five Passing Down the Formula for True Self-Worth

1. Media's Effects on Girls: Body Image and Gender Identity, National Institute on Media and the Family, 2002 (http://www.mediafamily.org/facts/facts_mediaeffect.shtml).
2. Ibid.

3. Laurie Mintz, lead author of the study and an associate professor of educational and counseling psychology at University of Missouri-Columbia; ABCnews.com, 30 October 2002 (http://www.abcnews.go.com/sections/living/Healthology/HSsupermodel_depressionson021029.html).

4. Survey conducted by the Vagisil Women's Health Center at the annual convention of the American Association for Health Education; 1998.

5. Alex Ayres, ed. *The Wit and Wisdom of Eleanor Roosevelt* (Meridian Books, 1996), 92.

Chapter Six: Raising Daughters Who Say "I Don't" Until They Say "I Do"

1. Center for Disease Control (http://www.cdc.gov/mmwr/preview/mmwrhtml/mm5138a2.htm).

2. *USA Today*, 3 June 2003 (http://www.usatoday.com/news/health/2003-06-03-teen-usat_x.htm).

3. Independent Women's Forum Study.

4. Kathleen Parker, "In matters of sex, things never change," *Orlando Sentinel*.

5. Larry Bumpass and Hsien-Hen Lu, "Trends in Cohabitation and Implications for Children's Family Contexts in the U. S.," *Population Studies* 54 (2000), 29–41.

6. For the past three years, as part of its Next Generation Program, The National Marriage Project has been conducting research into the attitudes toward dating, mate selection, and marriage among young unmarried adults. Last year the team reported on the results of a national survey of young men and women, ages 20 to 29. This year, the team took a closer look at a select group of young, heterosexual, not-yet-married men.

7. Center for Disease Control (http://www.cdc.gov/mmwr/preview/mmwrhtml/ss5104a1.htm#fig7); YRBS, 2001.

8. *Newsweek*, 9 December 2002, 61.

9. Neil Howe and William Strauss, *Millennials Rising: The Next Great Generation* (New York: Vintage Books, 2000), 200.

10. *The Guttmacher Report*, August 2001.

11. Howe and Strauss, *Millennials Rising: The Next Great Generation*, 201.

12. "Sex/Not Sex: For many teens, oral doesn't count," *USA Today*, 16 November 2000, front cover.

13. Ibid.

14. Ibid.

15. "Sex, Condoms, and STDs: What we now know," The Medical Institute for Sexual Health, Austin, Texas, 2002.

16. Ibid.

17. National Campaign to Prevent Teen Pregnancy.

18. *Seventeen*, January 2003, 114.

19. Ibid.

20. Ibid.

21. *Austin American Statesman*, no date given.

22. *Seventeen*, January 2003, 115.

23. "Facts & Stats-1," National Campaign to Prevent Teen Pregnancy, 2002.

24. Henshaw, "U.S. Teenage Pregnancy Statistics."

25. Ibid.

Chapter Seven: Dressed to Lure or Dressed to be Pure

1. *Brio*, September 2001.

2. *CosmoGIRL!* March 2001, 110.

3. *Complete Woman*, October–November 2002, 7.

4. Need source for *Teen Style* magazine.

5. Jessica Simpson, "Jessica's Corner" (http://www.jessicasimpson.com).

6. Nora Schoenberg, "Take It Off, Britney," *Time*, that is *Chicago Tribune*, 26 August 2002, 1.

7. Joyce Saenz Harris, "Innocence Lost," *The Dallas Morning News*, 10 June 2001.

8. Ann Oldenburg, *USA Today*, 24 August 2001.

9. Francine Parnes, "Dressing Down for Summer Worship," *New York Times*, 24 August 2002.

10. Barnes' Commentary, electronic database. Biblesoft, 1997.

11. Ibid.

12. Ricardo Gandara, "What girls wear, and what boys think," *Austin American Statesman*, 22 April 2001.

13. Emily Wax, "Parents Can't Bear Girl's Skimpy Attire," *Washingtonpost.com*, 11 August 2001.

14. *American Family Association Journal*, September 2003.

Chapter Ten: A Heritage in God's Word

1. *Ladies' Home Journal*, December 1948, 185.

2. Frank Harber, *Reasons for Believing* (Green Forest, Ark.: New Leaf Press, 1998), 73.

3. Paul E. Little, *Know Why You Believe* (Downers Grove, Ill.: InterVarsity Press, 2000), 77.

4. Bruce Bickel and Stan Jantz, *Guide to Bible Prophecy* (New York: Harvest House, 1999), 108.

5. "Study: Bible gives readers more positive outlook on life," *Austin American Statesman*, 13 November 2001; original source: *Newsday*.

6. Beth Moore, *Feathers from My Nest* (Nashville, Tenn.: Broadman & Holman, 2001), 155–56.

Chapter Eleven: A Heritage of Prayer

1. Bob Hostetler, 2003 (http://www.bobhostetler.com/writing/bestof003.html).

2. Author Unknown.

Chapter Twelve: A Heritage of Faith

1. Oswald Chambers, *My Utmost for His Highest*, October 30 (Philadelphia: Discovery House, 1992).

2. Barna Study (www.barna.org).

3. Author not sure of source.

Appendix: A Note to Mothers with Sons

1. Rochester *Democrat and Chronicle*, Pittsburgh (AP), 14 April 1992.

About the Author

Vicki Courtney is the founder of Virtuous Reality Ministries and www.virtuousreality.com, an online magazine for middle school girls, high school girls, college women, and adults. She is a national speaker and the author of several books and Bible studies, including *Yada Yada: A Devotional Journal for Moms*, *More than Just Talk: A Journal for Girls*, *The Virtuos Woman*, *Virtuous Reality*, and *Get A Life!* She resides in Austin, Texas, with her husband, Keith, and their three children, Ryan, Paige, and Hayden.

Other Helpful Web sites

vickicourtney.com—to view Vicki Courtney's current speaking schedule or find information about inviting her to speak.

virtuousreality.com—features online magazines for preteen, teen, college, and adult women. Check out this wholesome alternative to the anything-but-wholesome fashion magazines!

virtuousreality.com/events—provides information concerning upcoming Yada Yada and Yada Yada Junior events or about bringing an event to your area.

virtuepledge.com—sign in and join the virtue movement!